LIFTED BY THE SPIRIT OF THE MOUNTAIN: ARMAGEDDON AN APOCALYPTIC REVELATION

Chronicle 32

Panagiota Makaronis

KREA PREA Est. 2012

ISBN: 978-1-7644581-5-3

Cover design by: AI B3STOW (TM).
Editor: KREA PREA Est. 2012
Written: Australia Melbourne Victoria Craigieburn

Lifted by the Spirit of the Mountain

Armageddon an Apocalyptic Revelation

Chronicle 32

Is Dedicated to

Nikolaos Makaronis

A Rude Awakening, added with a divine true calling, the choices that were made, were made up. It was part of a bigger picture. A given trade, where there was no challenge worth the trouble.

It was part of a given fable, that served me well.

Forced to retrieve one more winning streak, before I hit that final spell. That one draw that became part of an angle that served me several. It ended with a bad hand, an omen to separate the old with the new.

The end of that Journey I once knew.

For the corrupts final verdict was nonsense a lie to cover up the truth.

Where I had to fight back, find a leeway towards the next freeway. A trace that will stand to deliver. A foundation about to collapse because time took its toll to consider the facts.

Time to step back, get back on track, face another force & hand the Corrupt a taste of their own remorse.

Amen

PANAGIOTA MAKARONIS

CONTENTS

Title Page

Copyright

Dedication

Epigraph

INTRODUCTION 1

CHAPTER 1 5

CHAPTER 2 15

CHAPTER 3 27

CHAPTER 4 39

CHAPTER 5 52

CHAPTER 6 66

CHAPTER 7 80

CHAPTER 8 94

CHAPTER 9 107

CHAPTER 10 120

About The Author 137

The Theatrical Melodia of my Life : Chronicle One 141

INTRODUCTION

Lifted by the Spirit of the Mountain: Armageddon an Apocalyptic Revelation; Chronicle 32.

A continuation of The Theatrical Melodia of My Life. Time to come to terms with the fact it is the end of Civilization as we know it. I have lived through many pitfalls, high and low. I can't help thinking I'm victim a classic, glutton for punishment. I keep going back for more not war, just to find peace.

The constant manipulation, Gaslighting, I must confess, has me intrigued. For those who are reprieved, have become part of a system that feeds off individuals like me. Just to hand messages to those who don't have information to give. But a good at observing and absorbing material.

Human Vampires; feeding off the gift. For the choices made, created a warning. The decision to clear the vision was made in the past led me to here, a presentation abundant but not clear. An expectation that served me an alleged miracle, a trial replacing the old with the new.

A forthcoming review, that had me set a final precedent. But yet again it served me wrong, it handed me the energy that has me face a failed trace. I was forced to hit back with a final vendetta at the end of that adventure. It sent me a message a well-deserved and desired impact to that praise.

It led me towards a challenge that had me foreclose a future event. Where the dream I was once yearned for, froze and I become morose. A nightmare yet to be served, for those who were corrupt were on my raider, trying to find ways to enter my realm; so, they become part of my Series.

The loss had brought forward a new solid ground a world unknown to me. A constant reminder the lie outdid the truth. An endless coverup by the corrupt to pressure me into failing, falling into impurities. Served me an angelic energy, a demonic field, it led me believe, the world was spiritual.

Humanity Holistically is a ritual, not only has it gone mad; it has driven us all into an oblivion. Trying to express my beliefs, while my experiences, held me hostage by the system. Having to come to terms with the fact those who are handling my affairs were pushing me towards shutting it all down.

I went through one journey to the next pretending. Everything I thought, had me embrace the Eye of Christ. Instead, I hit the Evil Eye followed by the Eye of the Tiger. Facing my Demons and trying my best to follow up on another Quest. Only to witness I hit an eyewitness requesting a do-over.

Just to find peace from a drama that was never-ending. Leaving one road open, and entering another hit an eyewitness, further, farther than I ever imagined. I was Gaslit about to hit a fit, just to give he who was corrupt, a chance to break and kick me out of my empty space; I call my comfort zone.

I'm not afraid to admit, I was young dumb, absolutely blind sighted. Assuming the dream I had will way me in, handing me the power to win every inning. I became a Target to those who were facing a true rude awakening; a mirror of themselves. I was entering the real world of an incurable disease.

The thought I won't be judged, was far from my mind. For those who judged were no better than I. I couldn't care less what they thought though. Yet again I was part of the same world and everyone I met were judas. There was not one person that will serve me properly, we were butting heads.

I made mistakes whether they were intentional or conventional it made no difference. It was what it was, and I was given no leeway just an ultimatum to please those who used me to cease. I can honestly say my clumsiness was part of a journey that had me return and press replay.

I was not aware it was one sided, my time was wasted, pleasing he who needed me. When it came to my needs being met; ease my pain. I was stuck in the middle of damn Bloody threat. A chain reaction that kept me guessing. Whether I was wrong or right no matter what I said or did, I was surprised.

Looking for answers; had me targeted. Is it the system that fails, or an enigma that leads you towards making the wrong decisions. A question had remained to be seen, where the power to return and devour; have you divide and conquer. When you hit your prime it's at pride, added with prejudice.

For the decision made, was not yours to begin with. Your presence is praised your existence is obscure, because they hit you so hard; they want you insecure. Your patience runs thin it hands the system a chance to push you in the corner. Angering you and killing your spirit, hoping you fail.

Those who hit run and harm you are truly Chronicle 32. Presenting you with a gift that keeps giving. If you run the risk and raise concerns it causes an effect and harms you, with a huge interference. A death threat added with a debt, handing you an invasion that will serve the corrupt a hold up.

If it does not meet the criteria of he, who has you cornered. You find yourself in comparison to the worst-case scenario. You end up causing effects cornered by the system. A control mechanism where one false move and you're holding on to a bad omen. A challenge that leads you towards a final.

The decision made on my end to play the game had me in admin detained. No freedom to release for in the end I was fighting a lost cause. The only way to state a fact was enter the corrupts challenge, cease the day. Watch the way the system collaborates, take it all in, count your losses and win...

CHAPTER 1

◆ ◆ ◆

Socialy Untamed

I fell into and trial an error a temperamental effect, that served me a tremor. A past influence had returned to hand me a final expense to that trace. It hit me when I hit an end of the race. It handed me a vendetta paused an effect, where I found myself in the middle of a troubled gateway.

The corrupt integrated onto a system, that had me face a congregation, to that conjuration. A mission that took me on a path that had me face a trace to that case. It caused an effect and put me on a gateway to heaven and on a pathway to hell witnessing my life evolve; a challenge I could solve.

Where I get in and face another whimsical admiration

from within. The gates of evil opened freely, giving in and harming me from within. Where the ceiling collapsed and I had no chance to release that beast. It forced me to repeat a given coincidental affair.

I had to hand the corrupt a chance to throw another flare in the air. Where I had to release that beast prepare myself for one more feast. Where in all honesty what remained spiritual handed me the incur to scheme another theme forcing me to repeat and replace a trace at the end of the race.

For the wall did not fall only the facts, for the energy that created a challenge; served me well. I was trapped by those who were attempting to put me through hell. Warning me the only thing that created the piece was the last thing that had me forced to sit back and repeat.

An anomaly come to fruition, it had me stalling afraid to erupt. Several were on my raider, hoping I would skip it and they would escape unharmed. Hoping I would leave it to chance, but all it did was harm me in advance. For the edge of reason claimed another season, stepping into a complexity.

It had me face a reality check; it caved in on the concept and served me a praise. An incredible hit that stated a fact, it caused an effect and pushed me straight off track. I landed in a role that warned me I was stepping into a hole. Left to encourage the corrupt to return repeat request another feat.

I was hit with a trace, the energy that stated it, had me face another case. It handed me the intrusion to hit back with a confession. After the trace had me face a trap at the end of the race. It was part of an enigma that served me a key, it gave me a second chance to delve into a given trance.

Feeding off the corrupt, for no reason had me on trial. For the right sight, had me face a phase, so when I reached my peak, the only thing standing was the last thing raiding mt head so I can get ahead. It had me remain silent. I became way too cautious in more ways than I could imagine.

For those who knew were invading in my privacy, all so they can get a glimpse of a future event. It was handing me a fight, a chance to step back on track and repeat after the fact. I hit a trend at the end of that trial, where I stood to be reviewed and every trace had me rescued.

I had to incur an invasive event; it took me on a path that had me face a trial. A revival to that survival technique served its purpose. It had me face an intension to that manifestation. Where I was on the edge technically trying to redo and reclaim an interaction to a game that served me well.

For he who used me to claim his purpose. He had me trapped trying my luck to get back on track. It was preventing me from renegading. Those who were interrogating me knew the truth; it had me on the edge. Torn in more than one direction, hoping I would never reach my destination.

I was handed an end to a result that served me an insult. Only to witness my goals were way out of line, and apparently, I was fooling myself. Even though my achievements had it first class, gold Pass grand entrance. It still gave the corrupt the pleasure to forbid me from entering with leisure.

The realm I created in peace, had me face another feast. For those who knew could not wait to release that beast and face me with a given to help me reveal revive and follow up on another dive. It had me causing effects and presenting the corrupt with a vision to hand me a composition.

No longer I was to invite he who knew and he who had a clue. For I was left to hit back with a case that had me face another trace. A given reason to repeat after that fact. It was part of a trace that served me well for no reason. For they used me to get in, ponder every thought from within.

It caused an extension to clear my name and claim my redemption with recission. All because the corrupt saw me as a threat and wanted to harm me so I never claim another tradition to the game. I had to release that beast. Face a feast forced to hit back with remorse catch up and claim the game.

It had me awaken from that forsaken expense; it forced me to endower. Release that beast that took me in and forced me to release that demon from within. I had to engrave a trace change that trend and challenge the corrupt in the end. That trial served me a dead end and led me to believe.

For that trace had me face a final review. I was given a good reason to encourage the corrupt to return and hit back for no reason. So, when I reach my peak, I could step into a trend and follow up on a new improved thread, the trace was a given, and the trend was not forbidden it was a given.

There was a document, a given warning, to have me step into the Omen. If I did not meet my quota, my light will be dimmed and the challenge given to the next of kin. But to my defence there was no one else to take my place and no fool was strong enough to put up and shut up.

The amount of chaos that was pushed towards my direction had me facing another manifestation. Feeding that dog a bone, had me Haunted at the end of that drone. There was a trace that had me convey a condition. For there was a bad day about to succumb, handing the corrupt their outcome.

It was handing me the impression they were serving that demon that was harming me. Where I was locked in helping he who wanted to harm me at every proposition. I was stalked left to hit the corrupt with a force that served me a cause. It had me trapped in the middle of a cause and effect.

It forced to release that beast, that served me a piece. I was on the edge left to interrogate forced to evaluate. So, when I elevate, I catch up and face another given, handing the corrupt the forbidden. The individual who had a clue used a method to harm me right through.

I was left to give in, save myself from the corrupts delusion. The misinterpretation was based on a past sacrament, leading me to a destination that will serve me well. It forced me to follow up on a mission that had me face another transition from heaven to hell.

Giving me the impression, I hit the end of that travesty a trial an error and a final dilemma. I fell into a heap trapped in the middle of the deep. Serving the corrupt a chance to release repeat and follow up on another distinction to that mission; it had me facing a final composition.

The urge for the corrupt to surge, had me saved. There were several on my raider stagnant to my development. It led me towards a journey that served me a trend. It took me in and had me trial a release to that beast. It forced me off the edge straight into a trace that had me on the edge.

A feast was prewarned; in the end of that piece, it caused an effect it had me revive a reification to that final manifestation. I am rising above and knocking down walls, hitting the ceiling that forced me off my pedestal causing the wrong effects and creating a challenge that had me resurrect

I had to reinstate another trace, at the end of the case, causing the wrong effects. The less we saw the better we create; it had me forced to hit back with love and hate. It led me towards a challenge that surely had me forced to break the system and feed of the mission.

The damages that were created by peace were corrupt. The only thing that had me face a trend from within, was the truth. There was no task; to embrace, only a leak to face a test to interrogate a vision to validate and follow up on a competition. Creating a mission at the end of the proposition.

The only way to give in was break the system and start fresh from within. There was no treatment, to evaluate or trace to parish. The truth set me free it gave me the energy I needed to invade all and present the corrupt with a final fall. An interrogation that will hand me the final investigation.

A trap that had me forced me to give in, forced to pry in the in the curse that had me vile, at the end of that trial. When I hit the end of that acclaim, the only thing that had me face another given from within was the challenge that served me a will to invite a Shepard in the village of sacrament.

Where the end of that trend the given was based on a trace, it had me face another force at the end of that cause. Giving me the impression I hit the end of that deception. Warning me the rest was history, the only thing that had me face a new improved trend; was a bad ending to that dread.

For the corrupt were too busy trying to investigate and carry on to the next. They gave me such a terror from within I had to face the facts force them off the tracks. Create a warning from within a yearning to give me the energy to feed off the journey that lined me for a winning streak.

A challenge to break the weak a trace to integrate as I interrogate, releasing that demon that forced me to hit back for no reason. It forced me to release that beast that had me forced to hit back with a curse that lined me up for a test that hit me when I hit the end of that trend.

There was no inning in the end of that terrible act of kindness. Only the edge of reason that had me forced to hit back and face another warning at the end of the race. For corrupt served me well it had me face another spell break the chain that led me off track straight into a terrible lie.

A feast to help me release, a thought that served me well. It was handing me the impression I hit the end of that foundation handing the corrupt famine. Damnation, that led me to the next destination. I fell into heap lined up for a warning at the end of that theme.

It had me scheme in-between, creating a challenge that forced me to disclaim another train of thought warning me I was left to embrace another trace at the end of the race. It had presented me with a brand-new curse at the end of that verse. I was off track, breaking that force.

It periodically left me hitting back with remorse. I had to hit back with a vision, cursing the corrupt at every proposition. It had me stepping into the unknown, hitting back with an incantation, to that next destination. I had to embrace cause an effect and hit the corrupt up with a trace.

I had to embrace, then compete with that made up story in my head I compelled by the lie. Because the truth did not serve me well. The one thing that had me face that vision to that destination from within was hit back. All while I face another trace feeding me lies at the end of the rise.

It served me well and presented me with an extension to that redemption. An infestation from that royal flush that left me facing another warning. Where only thing standing was the problem not the solution. The journey was to depart and revolutionise the next trace, at the end of the race.

It had me face another vision to the mission. I had to get in and follow up on a pointless affair. A challenge that had me claim a division to the game. Where I had to step up face another truth, so when I hit the end of that calamity the talent was not wasted it was part of the departed.

The impression was a lesson, the corrupt were lessoning the load. All by feeding off me and my creativity. It was hunting me down with unnecessary scrutiny. For the curse was part of the thirst to hit back and face a trace at the end of the race. For whatever was to come from that outcome.

There was no reason for the corrupt to harm me in the long run. It was based on a given impression to rely on the corrupts final manifestation. Just so I can catch up and face another trend at the end of that final. Just a given in, hit back with a brand-new allocation; to the corrupts final destination.

A trace that reminded me the only thing that had me forced to win was the last thing that restored my energy from within. Where the trace led me to replace and create a truth whole lot of individuals who are to confess. Facing a true reality to a journey that served me well.

A trend that had me, step into the unknown. Forced to Set it all free, break the silence and hand me a key. I had to trace trap and take the moment to feed off the energy that had me close one door and prepare me for one more flaw while I continue on my journey releasing that demon once more.

I was served a yearning, one false move and the energy that stirred the pot restored my head. It was heaving at me, so I never look ahead. Feeding off the journey that lined me up for a theme taming me in-between. It had me fierce scheming for another final meeting in-between.

CHAPTER 2

◆ ◆ ◆

There Is No Time For The Corrupt To Rise

I hit a final, I was nowhere near the end of that trend, it had me face a case. I had no choice but to return hit back and rejoice. I was given a reason to restore my energy and case that trace. A given point to return, face another warning just to force that cause and hit back with a final remorse.

It took me in and forced me to face another taste, a test that had me forced to redo acclaim and feed off the trend at the end of the test. A train of thought that made me see I was nowhere near the corrupts test. Nor did they carry a dynasty a level of revelation to hit back with a confirmation.

They worked in unison, stirred the world with there lies. They were creating a war cheating with a cause where they assumed they could hit back with an encore and face another trace at the end of the race. led me to revive another demeaning cause that had me hit back and face a trace.

I was hit in droves; preparing myself for another voyage when I realized the corrupt were on the path of monitoring my every trace that had me face another case. I hit the end of that method that served me a distortion to that distinction. I had to face a proposal to that violation.

It served me a warning, challenging me at every yearning. Haunting me while I was given a reason to attain another treason. The thoughts were unravelling the truth set me free it gave me the motive to stand clear and face another remedy. I was hit with a sphere at the end of that violation.

It handed me a vision to decline and feed off the mission. I was hit in-between stepped out of my comfort zone. Denied access forced to remain sanctum to a tradition that was not in violation in fact it was a given to hand me the ride towards a journey that served me well on the other side.

An awakening to follow up on a challenge that had me disadvantaged from the beginning. It brought me forward it led me towards a journey that had me state a fact. It created a piece and had me follow up on another relief. A trend that took over my journey and had me saddened again.

For no reason I was standing in for he who wanted to steal my key. I was on the wrong path, reserved for another trend reviewing what I knew. All while the rest remained earnest. I stood still started fresh and yet again I had no freedom nor foundation to process.

I was taken in followed by a string of events that took over my trace and recreated a new trend. It had me hitting a tradition once again. Reaping a reward stepping into a challenge that handed me the reason to follow up on a trace that handed me treason. Given a motive to face another trend.

That is when I knew I hit a dead end and the freedom that served me then had me start again. A constant reminder it was based on the corrupts final alignment. I was on the cusp trying my luck to hand the corrupt bad luck. A reason to follow up on past treason a stepping stone to the next lurch.

Trapped in the middle of a season that gave the corrupt a reason to hit me with a competition. It served me a road to recovery it handed me a clue and had me face another challenge. All while I was in the middle trapped in the trend that served me well in the end.

I had to face another trace skip that feast that had me foreclose another piece. I was taught a lesson just to give the corrupt a chance to reminisce and follow up on another gist. They screwed me right through, handing me the evaluation to promote me and push me off the edge.

I was left to repeat, lied to in the end, just to face another trace. It gave me a second chance to repel and feed off the corrupt all while I was given a reason to disclaim and feed off the tradition that had me forced to hit back with remorse. I had to reminisce feed off the trace and break the system.

All so I can continue to repeat another treason. All while the corrupt walked off, assuming the lie will hand them the truth. In fact, the trace was a given, there was a presentation that handed me the resignation. Just to break the corrupts mission, leaving them totally out in the cold; stark naked.

Have them frozen in mind, body and soul solid no trace no trend no foundation to pretend. Just a given reason for them to return and clear the mess. All while I cleanse my spirit and have them confess. They created a challenge to remind me of my loss leaving me struggling hurrying it all up.

All while they were on my raider, trying their best to hit me and run and have me forced to foreclose another outcome. The trend was uncanny the trace was presentable and those who were establishing a clue had me foreclose another review. Facing me with a key that had me stale mate.

It had me state another return at the end of that trend. It proved me wrong and handed me an extreme to that lead that had me forced to break the challenge and face another breed. Where the only thing that had me face another trace was the last thing that caused an effect.

It presented with an evaluation to restore my energy and hand me the end of that trend with a confirmation in the end. I was left to repeat and follow up on another trace at the end of the race. Taught a lesson and forced to repeat and follow up on another trace at the end of the race.

It will lead the corrupt towards a dead end, a curse that will have me hit back with remorse. It created a sense that had me forced to repeat and follow up on a heat of the moment. A challenge that took me in and served me well from within. It forced me to face a trace wasting my time.

It was preparing me for another trial a test that handed me an enigma. It had me word it in a way where every thought took its toll and everything that had me face another inning served me well from within helping me overcome another warning in the long run.

For that energy that faced me at the end of that trilogy warned me off the curse. It had me face another verse, stirring the pot and heaving at me every time I was handed a challenge that led me towards a journey that served me well. A willingness to help me find a way out of that skill.

It had me feed off the mirth that handed me a return. There was no laughter humour or fun no glamour or Glory on the long run. It felt as if I was being stalked warned of what was to come from that outcome. There was no trace challenge or treatment that was observing me.

It was an undesirable outcome that kept brewing. Where every time I was trying to rehabilitate and heal from the past the negativity was hovering over my head. It had me suffering in silence, so I lose my freedom, foundation and my head trying to get ahead. Trapping me so I turn and reveal a step.

Returning and hitting me with a curse, I could not reverse. I had no freedom to rehearse. I was left facing a reason to hit the corrupt back with treason. All because the trace was a case, I could not endower because the corrupt saw me easy and had me on the edge forced to pledge.

A task I could not erase had me face another trace. It led me to believe the only thing that led me on was the drama that served me wrong. Every follow up had me locked in, as if I was their trace to get in. When they realised, they were wrong they wasted all that time trying to remain strong.

It had me on the edge, trapped in a world that was not meant for me. I was taken for a fool served by those, who were corrupt. Tricking whom ever so I never get further. I was trying to fight off that demon that attached to my spirit. It was hard to repel, the need to repeat rebel put me through hell.

Even though I had the finger pointed at me; I could not accept that reality. For the trace and the drama unfolded and I once again hitting a dead end wondering what I did to deserve that review. The corrupt once again on the other end trying to cover it up with a trick they could not predict.

I was taught a lesson, left to the imagination, creating a piece that served me a validation. Where the only thing that served me well from within was the energy that created that key. A follow up towards that final degree became unworthy. A journey that served me had me reach my pinnacle.

I had to face the truth there was no liability to that scrutiny. I was given a reason to decline declare and face another treason. It was prewritten by a force forged with a conspiracy that had me facing another liability. One false move brought me back to reality a task that led me towards a hoarse.

Returning the favour, had me fighting for my life. It was creating a challenge that took me in and prevented me from regaining conscious awareness again. I was on the run rejoining to those who had me revealing another sentence to that tradition that forced me to hit back with admission.

There was no reasonable doubt it was played so well my words were twisted and I went through hell. I was on the edge preparing me for a faith less likely for me to succeed. I was on my path trying to make do with those who knew and he who had a clue. It had me face a final review.

Honouring that duel, reserved me a renewal. For the last thing that had face a new inning, cause an effect and create a deception that led me towards a journey where I was about to fail every revelation. I was waiting for the case to erase and the follow up to that trend portray a dead end.

I was to give in so the corrupt can warn others and hand me another challenge. I had to fight back from within. I had no chance in hell to press delete, for what I had was given. It gave me a chance to release a feast that caused an effect and presented me with a curse I could not reverse.

The world I entered was overbearing interrupting me at every serving. The corrupt were using me to steal a key and I on the other end defending honour and trying to avoid another siren. Where I give in and face that demon that took over my journey and wronged me for one damn reason...

A terrible truth had come to fruition, that is when I knew the corrupt were returning, for a competition. Here they were again, up and going the next generation waiting to return to belt me internally. Interrogating me assuming the worst will come and they will get their outcome.

Stirring trouble and pushing me off the edge; had me facing another enigma to that stigma. For the trace had me forced to replace and give in and prepare me for another win. Warning me, the only thing that had me forced to replace a trace was the last thing that handed me a threat.

It had me on the straight and narrow. Where I hit a road work towards a crossroad. To many delays blockages no one giving me a chance to relive my light. I was constantly bombarded with certain individuals who were forcing their way in trying their luck to break my spirit from within.

I had no faith; I lost my light the given momentum that had me rewrite my passageway. I was on the edge wasting no time because the corrupt had me face another given. A momentum that led me towards the forbidden. It hit me with an unregistered key, a challenge that served me a right.

It hit me with a final delight, just to delay the corrupt at every view. It caused an effect and trapped them in the corner to pay out a debt. Because apparently, they kept feeding and breeding forcing me and horsing around so

I hit back, God Willing. The only way they could repeat was trouble me.

They entered my realm unwelcome. With poison, passion and pressure, the constant reminder I was dumb deaf and blind sighted. I was done trying to get them to see sense, in the end I could not careless. I was left to pretend and face a death threat forced to hit back with remorse.

I was given a challenge taught a lesson left to believe the trace was part of a trend that had me sit on the perch handing the corrupt a dead end in the end. Where every section was parts that were missing. The curse was to reverse, and the trend was a dirty had me face another case.

It forced me to hit back with integrity. For what was to come from that outcome was too hard to bear. Because they hit me at my bare minimum I was left to hit back with a challenge to get me back on track. It had me face the end of that passageway waiting for the corrupt to surrender.

I had to haul and heave at he who warned me there was no trace at the end of that travesty cursed me at every dishonour, heaving at me whenever I had an itch waiting for me to glitch. All while I rise above that fall. I had been taught a lesson way too many times left to please those who heave.

In the end the world did not convince me otherwise nor did it give me a chance to dive into a trance. What it did was handed me that lead me to create a war in he who harmed me in spirit so he can breathe. I decided to take a chance create a trance and follow up on a feast.

So, when I caught up, I could create a trace that served me well at the end of the race. It was a warning a challenge that was yearning to be repaired and reported. For what was initially part of the clue, gave me a chance to repeat and follow up on another feat.

I realised there was no chance in hell I was coming back to repeat an upcoming beat. Because I hit the end of that trend that served me well it forced me to release an upcoming spell. Where the only thing that come to be, was that energy that served the corrupt their final eulogy.

It served me well it forced me to hit back with a faith less likely for me to release and more likely for me to find peace. All while I return and release that beast that failed me at the end of that lease. For what I was given was a challenge that took me on a road that forced me to hit back with a curse.

It taught me well it recreated a rehearsal; hit back with a curse I could reverse. It led me to a destination that forced me to repeat an evaluation. There were no cause and effects, the drama was part of an extension to that manifestation that served me a confirmation.

At the end of that destination, there was no common ground there was no feast and the pressure to release that beast had me foreclose a trend at the end of that forthcoming dead end. For the end of that trend, made me see there was no, first or last priority.

Just a common ground, to face me at my true reality. It was part of a challenge that served me a key, I had to repeat rely on he who established a challenge wording it so he can continue to feed off me It had me fed off warned of the trace that took its toll and had me face another case.

I had to fight release that beast. It had me face a trace at the end of that case, then release that upkeep so I can catch the corrupt ready to erupt. Where the only thing that had me withstanding, was the last thing that served me a challenge that handed me a key.

It gave me a second chance to hit back in advance. The irrationality to that stagnant was aligned to an affair that warned me there was no chaos to that trace. But a given reason to hit back with treason. I was given a familiar task from the past one that led me to break that trade.

It forced me to hit back and raid that concave. I was given a chance to hit back in advance focusing on all so I can rise above that fall. What a delay that handed me a dilemma, it gave me a second chance to face the corrupt at every tremor. It had me face an everlasting force, to that morse code.

Just so I can get a glimpse of a future, event an interest that was forthcoming. Forcing me to hit back with a test that failed me. I had to regain and present the corrupt with a dead end at the end of that game. Cause an effect feed off that defect. Given a reason to declare that train of thought.

Disclaim another cheap shot to the game, I had to rehearse and catch up just to was feed off the corrupt, a tread that served me a thought that caused an effect. It had me on the runner up. Rising above and beyond on the condition where I can get in remain strong and win another inning.

It was part of a trick that took me in and trapped me from within. Helping me get through was hard to do, it handed me was the truth; an end to that spin that took me in. How it was all handled was enough for me to see I hit the end of that trend that served me a willingness to hit a dead end.

The trace to that drama was a constant reminder I had to give in. Left it to that last minute handed me a moment to reminisce throw the corrupt a kick. Where they handed the money in advance where I get to reap a reward. I had to feed off the concept and create a better outcome.

A journey I can fix whenever the corrupt handed me a picture-perfect momentum. Where every method had me forced to hit back with remorse. Where only then I get a chance to break the cycle and prepare me for a thought that hit me at the end of that trend. AMEN

CHAPTER 3

◆ ◆ ◆

Praise The Lord I Found My Encore

I was taught a lesson left to repeat, pushed in the corner just to return and press delete. The method was uncanny the challenge denied, so when I looked within, I found myself hitting a dead end. Winding down while I continue to break the cycle and start again.

Never in my lifetime I thought I would have to stand alone and fight for my life. I was proved wrong by those who stood to repeat they gave me a challenge that had me on the edge about to uncover another turn of events. It created a test to give me a step towards the wrong direction.

The end, of that trend, taught me a lesson, left me to repeat and start again. I was proven wrong and taken for granted so the corrupt can remain strong. A dead end at the end of that trend, became apparent. The alleged, had me stand to deliver forced off the edge; ready to pledge.

Handed a chance to reveal a stagnant affair, significant to that road that had me hit the abode. Those who used me to get there had me reinstating facts. A given a reason to hit back with treason to get back on track. I gave in, caved in on the concept, hit the end the trend with a dead-end.

I was put in a position that gave the corrupt a chance to hit me in advantage. A challenge that had me propose another proposition to that position. They were to be taught a lesson and prepare me for an ending that was pending; not a trail that was never ending.

An uncanny trailer served me a demeanor. I was torn in more than one direction I had no choice but to hit back with redemption. They kept going on and every chance they got they remained idling waiting for me to come forward and hand them a key. Causing an effect and using me periodically.

It reminded me of the error of my ways. A rude awakening that had come my way and the only way to leave me unravelling a clue. It was to create a challenge and skip the corrupt right through. It had me on the edge lifting my spirit and following up on a pledge, reasoning with a trial and an error.

I was held at bay, causing an effect and feeding off the defect. A task where the corrupt stood still and wanted to feed off me so I can reclaim and tied down and silent to the game. It was part of a division to a game gambling my dream away. Until I fell into a rumour that cleared my name.

There was no tremor just trauma to that dilemma a drama to delay a challenge all the way. It handed the corrupt a dead end to that game. The only way out was to hit back with doubt and the only way to stop it was to cave in on the concept and create a piece that had me face another trick.

It was part of a tread, that led me to embrace another code. As I linger off and decode that mode, serving me the abode. It was part of an error that was handing the corrupt a dead end to that terror. Stalked by him who hit me with deception. Every task had me face a trace, handing me redemption.

For he who knew caused an effect and handed me a repetition, hitting me with admiration. I was given a choice that had me rejoice, a rude awakening. It had me face another enigma for deceiving me. I had to return and feed off the stigmata. I was left to embrace and warn the corrupt to give in.

It had me hit a happy ending, a momentum that surely had me missed. I was ready and willing to give in and take over that gist that had me forced to reminisce. It handed me the case that was cursed at the end of that verse. A race to the finish line that took me in and fed off me from within.

I was taught a lesson left to release faced another friction to that mission that had me warned I hit the ends of that scorn. The drama took over and handed me the interaction to face another abreaction. A rumour that handed me the edge of reason; so, I question every season.

A challenge that had me hit the divine. For now, there was no trouble no trace no rubble just a foundation to hit the corrupt with validation. For they could stand a chance to hit back in advance face me with fear a treason an ending to that forbidden mark. I was l left to hit back with a warning.

Leaving me wondering what the hell did I do to deserve that reserve, a final revelation, to that destination. An end to that path had me forced to hit back with a final mark. A first glance, an everlasting tradition that hit me with repetition. I was brought forward purely to reminisce.

It hit back and faced another trace, just to say the least, an emotion to that division sent me to a road of disposition. I could sense the reality to that trend kick in it hit me with a fright. It had me fight a dead end. Every time I would make a mark, I would be stuck facing another turn of events.

Here I was on again, wasting valuable time clearing a dead-end task. A risk that had me foreclose and feed off the trace that served me well at the end of the race. It had me test time trying to get out of that trace that left me gambling my light at the end of the race.

For what was to come from that outcome was not real. It was the corrupts way of covering up another heave at that trend that storm. It had me surrender give in and hand the corrupt a dead end in the end. For that trouble had me forced to hit back with remorse; that never come to fruition.

Every time I hit the end the only thing that served me well was the drama that put me thorough hell. The trouble I caused was paused, getting them to confess claiming it all to their favour. A trace that will serve me well, presenting me with a trial an error, a final vendetta. I was paying for that one too.

This chronicle will pay for that debt, fix every threat and put the corrupt to rest. Then have them compete compel turn against each other. All while continue to right my memoir through hell. The trace and the constant reminder I had no faith in humanity served me serenity.

I was not interested in what they had to offer. They took it to far; I found myself stepping into the unknown. Fighting off a demon who had been on my raider waiting for me to hit back. Forcing me to do things that made no sense to me. Pushed and prodded, hit to the point I had no trend in the end.

I had to give in, give up and not bother to win. Because in the end I had no freedom to pretend. No one was welcome, I could not understand why they kept pushing, me off the edge. They were pressuring me to the point they made me out to be the perpetrator, just to reclaim their thoughts.

The conclusion was and remained to be seen. I was set up left to release that beast, forced off the edge harming me, so I never pledge. I could not find peace nor release just cover up another feast. All because I had to follow up on my dream. Where I was used abused and left to amuse.

I refused to be reserved for the corrupts final serve. I refuse to return to hit back and feed of the energy that had me recreate a task that was about to harm me. I could not sense the trend come to an end for I had to follow up on an extension to that redemption that had me hold up the reception.

Because I was about to evacuate, nothing would come from it, for what was supposed to be, had facing an anomaly. I had no foundation no freedom nor a given reason to return for a treason. There was a challenge that had me restore my energy and feed off the silence that served me an alliance.

I was given a momentum to undo and follow up on another clue. It had me feeding off the trial the error and the final vendetta, just to close one door and open another. There was always a calm before the storm and the corrupt were on my raider waiting for me to fail so they can sail.

I had to release that beast that forced me to find peace. Just to return for one more release. My method was calm; the trace was part of a case a given momentum to hit me back with treason. I had to reclaim my thoughts, clean what mess was left to behind. Retreat catch up fight for my life.

The act of kindness had me overreact. It served me well and faced me when I hit the end of that trend that trapped me. I was in the action following up on a final scene in between. Where each score was an eye sore and each fight had me face another trace a given reason to hit back treason.

It had me on the edge returning for another pledge. I was looking from within just to catch the corrupt in the act of facing me and handing me a true reality. It was part of a systematic invasion that had me stranded for no apparent reason. A final interrogation to release that beast.

It forced me to find peace from that present momentum. It caused an effect and had me restore my energy while I resurrect. A competition that led me towards a deception, caused an effect and presented me with a final restitution to that resolution.

It warned me I hit a brand-new clue, a cycle of events that had me manifesting a brand-new review. It was forcing me to claim and follow up on another game. I had to remain silent while the rest claimed whatever truth come their way. A final investigation had me standing in the middle.

A constant reminder the corrupt were deliberately belittling me. It was about to hit me with a failed inning attempting to break my wing and leave me unjustifiably looking from within. It had nothing to do with my character reference. It had to do with the way I was served.

It had me hitting a final intention to break that redemption. I was left to suffer, remain strong, face my fear and soldier on. For whatever reason the only thing that served me a treason was a trap to hand me the resolution I needed to reclaim my truth and feed off the energy that took over.

It had me face a force, remind me there was no justification to that publication. I was validated without a warning left to disregard all, just to hand me a given yearning. Left to hit back inundated with information rising above and beyond. Leading me towards a destination of validation.

An uproar to that dedication manifested towards the wrong destination. It haunted me when I hit the end of that exhibition. An encore to that system failure failed humanity. It was part of a warning that led me towards a journey that served me a willingness to hit back with sturdiness.

Giving me the trace that served me a case that denied me access at the end of the race. A final review to have me step into the unknown; worthy and beknown. The energy that created the piece gave me a nervous feast. It led me to systematic involvement that served me a willingness to peak.

I was taught a lesson and left to release. The way I was treated by the corrupt had me absolutely misled and left to fight back and create a death threat. I was not letting anyone in, only the family member who I birthed and the way they played that was at risk too.

I could sense my reality hitting me with a technicality. A warning that served me a yearning and a challenge that had me forced to hit back with remorse. All because they were returning to turn that individual against me right through. No one was given a chance to give in, because I was already in.

How they played it, was absolutely astonishing. They used someone to rent next door attempting finish me off they had him abusing me every day; I was afraid to walk out the door. The only thing that created a win was keep up with the program try not to talk. Then let the healing begin.

The curse was a verse, given a first and last trace. A trust fund to help me, get in, in the end. It was part of a trick, a test of endurance to help me look ahead. A turn of event to help me process while I progress. There was a trap to lure me in and force me off the edge, so I never win.

I was to be a visitation to that next manifestation. For in the end of that trend the challenge was creative it had me forced to hit back and follow up on another given a challenge that had me face an evolution. A rough ending to a critical momentum that served me downside.

Conspired with whomever, to harm me under the raider, all by allocating and breaching a contract. Because they thought they could; in fact, the best it yet to come. For there is no challenge that does not have a final outcome. The intention to get me thrown off the edge for no reason was seasonal.

It was a trace that created a treason. They were on a mission trying to take away my will power. Hunting me down like I was about to hit Armageddon. Where the conspiracy became energy that served me well hitting me just before I was sentenced to an early grave.

It was part of a past life regression invalid deal that I suppressed. I had to deal with an ordeal that left me suffering in silence, just to overcome that trauma that was hitting me in the long run. It was about to rapture my spleen, if I did not follow that yellow brick road the end of that scene

Corruption verses Redemption, trying to crucify before I was given a chance to express and explain my success and what my plans were. If anything, they jumped to conclusions and hit me with confusion. just before I could encourage enclose and follow the path that saved me a resurrection.

The past brought me forward, and the present delayed. I was stuck in a time warp, trying to get out of that game. A challenge that made me see I was being used and abused automatically. The past journey was updated, the presented reinstated. I stuck back on track feeding off the impact.

I was up to date, creating a piece waiting for the war to be released. The informalities to that sacrament had me forced to hit back with remorse. I was given an outlet to restore my energy and prevent the corrupt from ever returning and hitting me with a formality.

It made me a victim to a presentation, that did not serve me well. It handed me an evolutionary, revivification to that destination. It had me untamed, ready to violate the drama that served me a restriction, to that manifestation. It had me forced to hit back with an involuntary investigation.

The thought, where I had to run and hide start fresh had me facing another threat. I was hitting a threshold, where the troubled doubled, because I was being fed of, whole. By he who was made out to give me, a challenge that served me the energy that haunted me spiritually.

The impression became an indication that every motive, handed me an investigation. It created a piece that served me a release and, in the end, haunted me so I never reach my potential. I was taught a lesson left to repeat for I had no reason to return and press delete.

I had to face a fear clear the air repeat and repel against he who used me to get through because it was he who harmed spirit not me. I had to face a fear follow up on a scheme redeem another theme revive another trace get back on track break the system that had me face another repetition.

I had to start again, follow up another trend. For the corrupt were to use me as bait apparently. I was hit with a trace served a trend left to repeat and repel in the end. It had me for returning to clear that space that handed me poison at the end of the race.

It was feeding off me waiting for me to fail so I never sail. The drama was causing effects it had me face another trace, leading me to a destination that created a piece a final trend that had me hit a dead end. I had no interest in the corrupts final. It was a competition to compel every mission.

Where the interruption became my interrogation opening a new door to the next destination. The conclusion added regret, I was reaching out for help, only to witness I hit a final restitution; nothing but a regret from that debt. I refused to be abused and be tormented by the past.

It had me revealing a challenge that was burdening me. Assuming that method will give them a chance to steal another key. Even worse return the curse trying to steal my energy by latching on to me and feeding off me and making life a living hell. I did not know who until recently.

He who was feeding off me was latching on to me like a vulture. He had used method created predators to undo and screw me right through. I had to create a curse to humble myself so the corrupt can back off. But all it did was give he who knew a chance to catch me in the act.

For telling him how I felt was not part of that fact. It was part of a tact that brought me forward and pushed me off track. Until I found myself, forced to hit back with remorse, the only thing that will bring me a new beginning will be the last thing that will have me face the facts.

I was hit back with a challenge to release that beast and follow up on another feast. I had that one energy that undid and underwritten while I pledged. I tried to defend my honour only to have the corrupt sneak up on me return the favour torment me with a given.

An accusation that served me the right, manifested just before I hit an encore. For whatever come my way declined, for the corrupt were on my raider warning me to keep inline. There was always a challenge that had me press replay. Creating a war in my peace to help the corrupt find peace.

The corrupts were repeating and deleting an allegation handing me the right to decline that case that was manifested by him who created a war in my peace trapping me in the corner so I never peace. I was bombarded with information to allocate and follow up on another accusation.

CHAPTER 4

◆ ◆ ◆

The Honorable Encore

Before I had a chance to hit back with an
improve. I was hired to hit back with an
expose to clear my name and call it a day.
But the corrupt had other ideas and I was
back loaded with work that served them well
they locked me in and put me through hell.
I had no freedom to recreate a decision.

It had me sit back and twiddle my thumbs, waiting to be called up. Ready and willing to face another corrupt. A trace at the end of the race, had me on the edge ready and willing to pledge. Where the corrupt saw me as an easy target. I was facing a wrong move giving the corrupt a chance to confess.

They had to dive into a trance, wasting my energy in

advance. The challenges that took me in had me compel compress delete delay and pressure me all the way. It hit me silently on the move wasting valuable energy trying to complete a task and follow up on another trend.

I was given a chance to receive then condition the mission so I can breathe. I had to break the cycle and retrieve, then when the time come the journey was outdone. It had me face another trial and error and a final vendetta. It gave me a second chance to hit a challenge that served me a well.

I was on the edge trying my hardest to pledge, the trap became impossible to deal with. I was forced to hit back with remorse. I had to break the chain forced to hit back and face another brave move it gave me presentation that led me towards the wrong destination.

I had to trace that case that caused an effect; it had me forced to hit back while I resurrect and feed off the debt. In the end of the race there was a constant reminder I was always on the lookout and on the other end facing another revelation to the next destination.

I was waiting for the energy to repeat repel and finalise that spell. I had to repeat reclaim and follow up on another game. The choice was to have me rejoice and the drama foresee another warning. A test that had me replace a case, a desire to put me through the ringer was replaced.

It had me give in and face another inning. I was having a moment, a challenge to recreate a release to that beast. It had me redeem another scheme in between. I was seen as an easy target and the innovation to that motivation had become part of a key. A challenge that made me undo a review.

I was taken for a fool left to hit back and finalise that

remote. It had forced me to hit back with a momentum that served me well. It gave me a chance to see the corrupt had conspired to harm me while they were wronging me. I had to see the error of my way, and undo that clue.

I had created another anomaly to that sacrament that was about to serve me. It had come to my attention the corrupt were returning for a reincarnation. I on the other end serving them a final dead end the one thing that had me face another trace and present me with a curse I cannot reverse.

I had to rehearse; I was given a reason to come first. It gave me a second chance to feed off me in advance. A chance to release that beast and face me with a feast. Hinting to the rest; where the journey was a contest and I was heaved. Lining me up for a trend in the end of that final dead end.

I was innocent the trial was over the raider to that dependency had closed. Not only I caught the corrupt red handed but the trace had me forced to hit back with remorse, hitting them at every cause. I got a chance to release that beast that had me follow up on another final feast.

Feeding off my energy was giving the corrupt a chance to save themselves while they belt me in advance. Creating a trace that brought me synergy, it had me release that beast that forced me off the edge straight into a curse I could not reverse rehearse nor even come first.

During the writing of this scripture, I went back to where the trauma began. Trying to make sense of what I did to deserve such a bad name. Only to see my name was not part of the game, it was the fame. Even then, I could not condition the mission, because I hit a final competition.

Only to realise I entered and met an individual who was greedy and wanted to steal my key all because that individual was competing with me it forced me of the edge ready to declare decline and feed off the trauma that had me face another trace, at the end of the race.

It was outdated and I was outnumbered, based on my journey and my experiences updated. It created a rule that forced me to hit back and follow up on another cruel rude awakening. How I perceived Humanity within that social gathering made me out to be a fabricator.

For that interrogator, who was instigating another trace to that case; had caused an effect. It had me repeating another cause that will alarm he who was forced to push me off the edge, straight into a ditch. It had me feeding off the incurable debt, that handed me a purity to that inferiority.

It gave me a huge meltdown a challenge that served me well. Not only had I experienced the curse firsthand, but everything that caused that new beginning broke the chain. It had me face a new improved task a trade that caused an effect and brought me back to reality.

All while I caught up and faced a debt, to that death threat. It had me entertaining the corrupt in my domain. I had to reverse that trend that had me face a dead end. For the last message caused an effect it gave me the entrance to that domain that led me off the edge straight into a new strength.

It had me wasting it all, facing a royal flush. A given reason to belt the corrupt for one more season. It had me stepping into a road that served me a rule, it handed me the energy that led me to repeat repel and push the corrupt in the corner so I can continue to brand that key that was stolen from key.

A brand-new spell a case that had me forced to rebel, it gave me second chance to belt the corrupt in advance. For that measure that forced me to break that curse, had me face a true reality so I can continue to come first. I was forced out the door waiting for the corrupt to belt me once more.

I was taken for a fool left to repeat and rebel against those who put me through hell. For that pathway that forced me to cave in on a brand-new scheme was part of a survival technique that led me to play the winner to a game that was written and published by me.

Once I rise above and beyond that call back it handed me a recall to help me get back on track. My name kept getting tarnished by those who were varnished. They came first I came last and the fact I was the chosen one gave me the reason to repeat and forced to hit back with remorse.

They found me easy in the midst. I was hit with a deception that had me rise above that fall. It had me on the runner-up. Pushed me off the edge so I never rise above that fall. My journey Wholistically has been tarnished because of it. It stated a fact and left me stagnant to my development.

Not only had I seen the light and everything that served me had me yearning for another serving. Testing the patience of those who convey and follow up on a gamble. Waiting for me to press replay had me face another bad day. The journey was over and they had me a Jehovah.

The only way I could challenge the corrupt was cover up

a warning. It was part of a trend that had me face a dead end in the end. It was a pointless affair that had me step into a trace, where I get in lead the pact faces another trace key in and force the corrupt to give in, at the end of the race.

I was given a challenge that forced me to repeat, then return the favour and press delete. The corrupt were out of line, it gave me a second chance to heave hit back and face another impact. I was taught a lesson left to fight back in advance, so when I caught up, I could give in.

Interact with those who used me to get in face the fact to those who stir the pot and give them an ending that has been pending. I was on the trace to that event that had me forced to hit back and vent. A challenge that had me whinge from within. Left to repeat repel and press delete.

All while I prepare myself to get through hell, where the drama had me ascending. It was following up on a clue that served me a willingness to step forward and protect my spirit right through. Assuming heaven was better was not part of that vendetta it was part of that closure.

An entrance to an unknown pitfall. It gave me a second chance to face the trace that served me a willingness to repeat and remain silent to those who were vigilant. A given opportunity to follow up on a journey that served me well at the end of that forthcoming spell.

I was taught a lesson a given reason to repeat repel and

feed off that treason. A trace that forced me to hit back was becoming obsolete; I had to press delete while the corrupt remain idling. It had me face another trace a given reason to hit back and propose an ending that was pending.

I was given a reason to follow up on a betrayal. But the impact to the trouble was so huge it got to the point the drama was part of a given. It had me repeat repel and face an incoming development. The amount of creativity that forced me off the edge had me face a reason to hit back treason.

A pattern of energy that served me a lack of synergy, took its toll. The number was huge and I was served a brand-new role. A challenge that handed me a risen momentum to that trend had me seek find and follow up on a brand-new skill. A truth to that endeavour that handed me a vendetta.

I was served well in the end. I was taught a lesson; a valuable one in fact. I was left to repeat that thought pattern that had me on the edge of returning for another pledge. It took me in and had me face another vendetta that led me toward a trial and error. Even though the truth went through.

There was no time out I was handed doubt a challenge that will serve me well. I was given a reason to face another review. The impact was huge the drama was renewed; I was stalling long enough to know the trace was a given and I was showed the long haul before I took it all in.

I was given the energy to face another trilogy. I gave in where the impact was so hard I lost my will power to get in and win. Tried my hardest to harvest for the trend was based on a dead end. It served me well in the end. I was pleased and the corrupt were applauded for hitting me with ease.

Where the only thought that come forth was the last thing that served me well, from within. A challenge that took over had me face another risen praise, from that case. It had me fast forward to the next trend in the end. A task that took me in faced me with a dilemma from within.

The energy that created the piece forced me off the edge. I was given a trace that had me forced to heave so when I saw the energy face me it hit me with a cause and effect it forced me off the edge straight into a dilemma that had me hit the end of that tremor.

Every apparent momentum faced me with energy that served me a well. Each defective spell caused an effect and presented me with a challenge that brought me forward. It had me feed off the trial that had me repeat and hit back with denial. The error and the final vendetta had me remain vigilant.

All while I was given a reason to claim, break the system and start again. It forced me to redo and return for an admiral review. For that that chance to deny me access in advance was a given. It was a brave move, hit and served with whit, it had me on the edge returning the favour.

It had me repeating that pledge, that served me a willingness to hit back and face another tremor to that vendetta. I was lined up for a true rude awakening. It hit me well when I hit the end of that trend. It led me to believe the drama was part of a trace that served me well at the end of the race.

At the end of that test, it forced me to remain silent. I was to start again hit a review then follow up on a clue. It had me denied access right through, even though there was no groundwork, the challenge was stagnant. There was no challenge worth the troubles no trace worth the case.

I was given a reason for me to return for one more season. It was part of a trial an error and a final vendetta. I was on the edge returning to reframe the corrupt again. It was part of a clue that had me fight back and face a review a given reason to repeat, reclaim a rumour trace at the end of the race.

A destination that released that beast forced me to repeat and repel. It was handing me a forthcoming spell. An official trace to that case. An informal investigation was open and the corrupt took me in and attempted to sabotage my win. Handing me the opportunity to get the upper hand.

I was to return and break the chain completely. It had me generalising the truth and preparing me for a final frontier had me on the edge ready pledge. I was given a reason to replace it with a trend that served me well in the end. before the corrupt served me the reason to hit back with treason.

At every division the corrupt had a vision, because every final admission became apparent and the only way to catch up was report repeat and hit the corrupt at the end of that trend. A trial an error and a final vendetta, hit a review and gave the corrupt a second chance to hit back with treason.

I was left to return and face a warning; it served me a yearning. I was given a challenge that had me return so I can claim and catch the corrupt hitting me and running at the end of that forthcoming event. It was to hit the corrupt with a four-leaf clover. Causing effects hitting me with a defect.

For what it was worth the trace had me forced to hit back with cause. I could not have come at a better time. It had me face a trace the one that was given to me before I had a chance to give in. I was hit in advance. It was a given reason to release that reassurance; it had me face a final degree.

Instead of what could have been, had me face a trace. Instead of what is to come I was to face a given, a reason to force my way in and hit back with treason. The trace had me face an extreme scene a challenge that forced me to repeat and report an ending to that trend started again.

I was given all clear, reserved the right to repeat a given reason to return and press delete. For the final had come to fruition, hitting my intuition. For some reason I could sense foul play, my spirit had a moment of despair where I was given a cleanse and chance to cause an effect and start fresh.

Where it caused an effect and forced me off the edge purely to allow me to see I hit a final priority. I being tarnished by the corrupts mess, one that was creating an entertainment in my head.
They entered my realm unwelcome, trying to feed off my spirit so I don't see the purity in humanity.

has to offer society. to the next proposition, it had me face a presentation. It took me in, forced me to please my spirit from within. Every allegation handed me a force to band that glamourous hand. A fall out that could have been avoided, if I had known the corrupt were running the show.

It had me giving the corrupt a chance to belt me in advance. It was stored and kept brewing until the corrupt found a way in and attempted to face and feed off me from within. I was led to believe that the lie was part of a truth it had me face a reality that led me to become recluse.

Facing the world now had become a trauma, that served me well. Not only I adapted to what was handed to me, but what was to come was way too easy. It brought me the foundation that had me face another reincarnation. The allegations were created by truth it had me hit the end of that trend.

It served me the willingness to upkeep, start fresh. Delete, delay pushing the corrupt in the corner all the way. I could not accept nor state the truth; it had me foreclose and create a challenge to help me through. Every time I was forced to hit back the foundation to reserve was part of a debt.

A follow up on a gift to get back on track fed off the drama. A trauma that forced me to repeat. It had me face a trace, deleting and delaying it all; just so I can rise above that fall. As if I did not enough troubles to overcome the corrupt were on my raider stirring the pot hitting me with an outcome.

A key I created was stolen from me; it had me troubled with unity. As if I was chosen to please those who were entitled to an opinion. In the end the drama hit hard. The only way out gave me a chance to get in, feed off the trauma that served me the willingness to fight for the truth from within.

I was to decline that break and leave it all to chance. I was to declare and follow up on another trace. It was part of a given to hand me incantation, a trace that had me forced to hit back with an evaluation. I was taught a lesson left to repeat warned of the creativity that served me.

For the willingness to return and face another trauma.

It had me return to release that upcoming event, had me sense my true reality and what was coming next from that final technicality. For that task was a dead end in the end. It was handing the corrupt one more chance to attempt to pretend.

A challenge that had me face a given. Where every trace had me forced to hit back and prepare myself for another final admiration. It was forcing me to return and reclaim a given momentum. A trail an error and a proposal to give me the power to hit back with an immense trace.

All while I divide conquer devour and face a given. A task forbidden, just to get in state rearrange and follow up on a given and remain loyal at the end of the game. While I watch it all backfire where I come out the other end innocent once again. Tring to find peace while I travel to the next thirst.

CHAPTER 5

◆◆◆

The Harmonic Entrance

I was taught a lesson, once again, left it to the imagination. A challenge that saw me reliving a dramatic effect, had me pointing the finger at the wrong direction. It was harming me at every manifestation, not only I was given all clear but behind my back and closed doors.

The interruption to that manifestation, became unclear. I was on the edge trapped in the middle of a feast that had me win every ungrateful method for every time I entered the truth the challenge that followed had me reclaim another trust issue to a game that warned me, I hit the end of that domain.

I was facing a deformity to that normality. It created a

challenge that made me see clearly. The beast that was created by force had me fight for the truth. I was hit back with a kindred spirit that forced me to reclaim another division to a game that had me on the edge, starting again.

It forced to give in and pledge at every follow up. It was handing me the inclusion that violation that varied. Every institution had me facing a release, so when I caught up to that trace the only thing that forced off the edge was the last thing that was withstanding from within.

For the first thing that come to mind was the last thing that had me rebranded and frozen in time from within. It forced me to regain that intellectual momentum that faced me when I hit the end. For the internal abuse that broke my vision praised me at every composition.

For corrupt were planning an event from an aged old game. It had me stand my ground then pray to that demon who preyed on me to let it be. It was to let me go, follow up on another show because it was he who forced me to release and follow up on another piece.

Where I had to claim my thoughts and catch up with an internal bliss a cover up to release that beast. I had to get back on track every step of the way. Release that beast that forced me off the edge. Only to witness I hit an eyewitness a Humanitarian who faced me with an assumption.

They handed me a clue; it was part of an investigation

that led me off track straight into the narrow. No neglect no freedom to fret just the outcome to hand me the energy that served me well forcing me to break that class act that handed the corrupt a chance to face me in advance.

It gave me a chance to look within and follow up on another win. Assuming he knew more than I but in fact he was forced to hit me in the third eye. Assuming that will break me, but in fact it served me well and saved me hunting him down handing him the intern to that evaluation.

Pointing the finger at he who saw me as an easy target. Every thought forced me to hit back at the last resort. It had me returning for a yearning. A trend that had me face a warning. A loss forced me to hit back, with a pointless, act. A chance to face my true reality, feeding off the drama in advance.

I was led on trapped in the middle of a long-term effect; it had me face another troubled thought ahead. A given momentum that will hand me a clue it will force me off the edge straight into a ditch. It was breaking the silence giving me the power to undo and devour.

Despite the fact the corrupt were working in unison to push me off track. The service I was handed gave me a chance to revoke and carry on to the next step forward. I was led on and led to believe that the drama was based on a case that was turned against me.

Instead of allowing it to continue, I was forced to hit

back with remorse. I was locked in, fed off the drama that served me well from within. An enigma that was given had me finalising the trace a force that led me to hit back with remorse. For drama that served me the power to proceed harmed me.

It prevented me from repeating a failed attempt in-between. It forced me off the edge straight into a ditch, feeding off the release that forced me to reclaim a division to the game. A chance to return and hit the corrupt in advance led me to believe that the trend was too hard to portray in the end.

For the journey was uncanny and the trace was too hard to replace. I was being wrongly accused abused, left to suffer in silence so the corrupt can continue to prosper. I was up and ready to face a new reason to claim a deportation. Forced to hit back with remorse, I was hit for no reason.

All so I can get back on track, because the corrupt saw me as an easy target. I was torn left to re-appeal report repel and face another trace to that case. A reason to push the corrupt in the corner and hit back with treason. It had me feed off the off the drama and the damages the corrupt created.

Leaving me guessing wrong and having me get back on track with the old, start fresh and step forward and face another anomaly. For that trial that error was created intentionally to mix and match challenging me to get back on track and face another impact.

Purely to get me to fail, face a trace replace and break the cycle. It had me return for an everlasting trace at the end of that trend. Forced me to repeat and face a given reason to start fresh. Feed off the trial the error and the final vendetta. A chance to break the chain that was hitting me spiritually.

A final dilemma that caused an effect, forced me off the edge. I had to face a competition clean up the mess break the tradition, force my way in heaving at every final upkeep. I was waiting for the corrupt to give in and prepare me for another win. It had me at the end; pretty sure of myself.

A test that forced me to challenge the corrupt had me step into a new review. It saw me face an entrance that took me in and broke that trend from within. I had to repeat repel force the corrupt into hell so I can continue to heave while the rest face an energy that will cause me to breath.

I had to cause an effect and cast a spell, a challenge that had me break the trend and face another dead end. For they assumed they could perceive give in and finalise that energy that haunted me from within. I had to restart face another trace and follow up on another key.

All because the journey I was on; was way too cold. I was forced to hit back and break the chain. For the cycle to remain vigilant to the game was incredibly wrong. It was unravelling my head a given reason to follow up on a treason. Hitting me with an allegation, that will force me to break that trait.

There was no faith left for the truth was designed to push me off track. So, I cannot see light, project or fight back, because I was handed a challenge that was harming me and leaving me branded. All by he who knew and he who took it all in tried to feed off me so I he can get in and win everything.

A disconnection to that spirit hinted to me I hit a final anomaly. It was part of trend that caused an effect and had me feeling the uncomfortable momentum that was not meant to succumb that final outcome. It brought me a glimpse to that final feast it had me face an anomaly to that trend.

It had me face a failure release that beast that had me forced to hit back and finalise that piece. In the end I had to face another trace a given reason to break the cycle and follow up on another give a point taken and received holding on to a second coming. A goal that had me face another challenge.

In the end, the race was a given, a reason to decline and declare another mission to that deception. It caused an effect and faced me at every exposure. A follow up on one more theme before I was given a chance to undo and face another reification to the next destination.

For what I thought was part of my imagination, was actually not the case. It had me manifesting a resurrection from a past manifestation. The turning point was, when I was burning the pages. Hitting the corrupt with a final admiration. For that energy that forced me to hit back was silent and deadly.

With a burden on my back, a task that had me face another trace. It had me back on track troubling the corrupt and following up on another trap. There was no indication nor a validation just a reminder I hit a hold up. A method that had me forced to revive, revolve fight back and solve.

It had me feed off the trend that had me forced to start again. Facing a brand now role so the corrupt can continue to force me to hit back with an interlude. A joke I was about to evoke, just to find hope from a delay that had me press replay. Put on standby an adventure to recall a day to remember.

I had to make sure there was no encore. I was about to face another trace a given reason to force me off the edge. A challenge that had me face reality. Forced to recruit, face a given to give in and follow it up with a test of endurance, preparing me for a win. A given to hit back with treason.

I was trying my hardest to repeat and follow up on a trace. I was on the mark trying my hardest to give in and follow up on a given. A challenge that took me in and faced me from within. I was on the edge trapped in the middle of a composition, waiting for the corrupt to hit me with a competition.

I was led on, left to repeat create a piece that had me

forced to hit back with remorse. It was a hint that served me well and forced me to reclaim and remain silent to the game. It put me in a position not worth the energy waste. It served me a proposition, as I faced a final interrogation.

In fact, it was the journey that had me reliving the nightmare. Served me an ending before the new, had me face a challenge. A reminder I hit that sanctum simultaneously. Without having to put up or put out or even face a trace. Because the challenge was too hard to replace that trace.

All while the rest forced me to progress. It had me breaking the silence and harming my spirit, so I never face another trauma. An enigma that will harm me at the end of that trend. It was aligning me for a feast that had me face that beast. I had to repeat and when the time come press delete.

All while I envision the next competition, a challenge that had me face a new mission. It had me creating an expose' to the corrupts familiarity. I chose a challenge that had me chasing a dream, that served me well. Just to give in at every spontaneity in-between.

A challenge that had me step forward caused an effect, it had me face a defect. In the end I was tight left to fight back and regain conscious awareness again. A lesson lived and a lesson learnt had me wasting valuable energy trying to repeat repel and face another upcoming spell.

It had come to my attention the corrupt were on my raider, hitting me with redemption. It was a witch hunt they were on the prowl looking for that fix, to feed their hunger. All while I enter the corrupts deception feed them nothing but redemption. All while I watch hell freeze over.

It left me to repeat another investigation, just to prove that the corrupt were ganging up on me. I had no idea I was being hit with he who knew nothing but assumed he knew everything in fact they were torn given a reason to hit back with an everlasting trap. I could sense it all come to fruition.

They were waiting for me to fail all while interrogating me at every scale. It had me fighting for my life while the rest were trapped in a trend hitting a dead end. For I was given a reason to feed off the treason. This time I stirred the pot angered the lot pushed them in the corner watched them all rot.

A trace that had me face another trend in the end of that dead end. Where my imagination took the best of me it hardened my spirit fed off my soul took me on roller coaster ride from heaven to hell. My imagination was creating a force to hand the corrupt remorse.

I was on the mend, from failed dead end, fading away and hitting me every step of the way. A trace that served me well and handed me an induction to that manifestation became part of a loyal investigation. For those who fed off me took it all in and had me heaving at every whim.

I did not have a chance in hell of repeating a thing, because every thought that held me down forced me to win. For, what I had was a final a given, a reason to hit the corrupt back with treason. I did not have the time nor the pleasure to release that pressure. It all started to overload and I exploded.

Waiting patiently for the corrupt to react had me face another feast. It hit me with a final piece. It caused an effect led me to repeat repel and push me in the corner and feed off me while I bit the bullet and face another trace. It took the role play of a keeper, who belted me all the way.

They ran hid and fell into a heap, waiting for me to fail and attempt to break my spirit. All so they can rise from the dead end. Because their demonic ways were given a chance to face me in advance forcing me off the edge, so I claim the game dispose from that mission and start again.

The reason was uncanny their point was unravelling I was not happy. I hit an ending that was pending and a faith that was less demanding. I realized too little to late I was leading the pact and losing the drama that forced me off track. It was causing effects hitting me with a defiant test.

A traumatic event that had me face a trial and error at the end of that tremor. I was hit with treason trapping them in such a mannerism; hoping I give them an aneurysm. It will hit them and feed them disaster at every measure. The constant reminder I hit a wrong move was the end of that trend.

It had me face a trace a given reason to decline face a final admiration. That kindred spirit that forced me off the edge, straight into a ditch had me reminded the curse was reversed, the trend will end and I will overcome a nasty outcome. For that personal vendetta ended in a strategic event.

Where it felt that I was being ganged up on and the only way out was hit a dead end then start again. For that a demon was fighting for his life waiting for me to save him warning me every thought was everlasting and every trace forced me hit back with haste.

I was facing a challenge, that was undeniably at ease. There was no trace the given momentum had me replace and face another case. The malice became part of a challenge that handed me a force I had no choice but to hit back with remorse. The energy that had no discretion finally hit me.

An ending I could relate to, had me facing a never-ending response. It forced me to hit back with a verse; I could not revive nor substitute for another trace to that case that gave me permission to erase that given vision. All because I was left to hit back and face an enigma to that stigma.

I to remain observant to a game that had me face another resurrection to that deception. All because every challenge had me face another trend in the end. The corrupt were holding me to ransom assuming that will encourage them to return and hit me with a vision; that served me a competition.

All so I can cave in on the energy that served me the willingness to win. Where every trace had me forced to hit back and face a release to that beast. It was hitting me at the end of that feast. I was given a random response, to hit back with every curse; that served me a willingness to come first.

I was on the mend, feeding off the trap that had me forced to return and start again. It was part of a clean way out leading the blind suffering in silence so I can claim and follow up on another game where every thought had me face a trace where every follow up had me feast off the beast.

A class act that had me face that self-doubt. I was torn in more than direction releasing that demon that returned to hit me at every final destination. It was part of a pointless affair that took me in and broke me from within. I was on the edge ready and willing to hit back with a trace.

It was restoring my energy at every case. Unravelling my head as I was taken for a ride so the corrupt can subdivide. Just so I can catch up condition the mission and face another enigma at the end of that stigma. For every manifestation I had to claim that destination with a given permission slip.

I had to hit back with admiration, thoroughly looking for ways to exempt and accept liability. For what was and what could have been; had me facing the end of that trend that had me forced to pretend hit back and start again. It was a follow up to next review a humble heroic momentum.

For that journey served me a sanctum. For what it was worth and for what was to come. The angle was set in stone, and the outcome was not as incredibly aroused nor astounding as it was meant to be. Because I hit the mark completed my task, restored what I thought was the end of that trend.

It had me in admin, starting again creating a dead end. A trial and error and a final vendetta.
Because it was set in stone and I had no idea I had to chase up and finalise that rude awakening. Chase the case trace that trend force a new feast and start fresh again.

A chance to roam, handed me a challenge to repeat and repel. All while the corrupt return and press delete and put me through hell. I had to return smash that solid rock and remain silent while the rest follow up and feed off the trace that had me foreclose and create a better outcome.

It had me face the wrong fascia, leading me towards a destination that had me repeat one more dangerous enterprise. Where I get in and create a challenge from within. It warned me I was nowhere near the corrupts final revival. Because every thought hit me with the last resort.

CHAPTER 6

◆◆◆

The Medieval Charm

I was in the middle of a challenge, that handed me the key. I was to release that demon, that had attached to me. It was part of a given a challenge that was forbidden. Where the only way out was part of that upcoming doubt. I had to accept defeat, follow up on another journey and press delete.

It was preventing the corrupt from attempting to return, repeat and reclaim a new lead. The conclusion was every validation hit me with confusion. The journey was untamed the trace rearranged, every comment given was part of a final written report that served me a presentation.

It was part of a destination that faced me with a brand-new breed. It had me face a condition to that mission that forced me off the edge straight into a proposal that led me astray. I was being hounded while the corrupt were grounded hitting an ending that had been pending for a while.

For that reason, the conspiracy became part of a treason. The betrayal was part of a final trend; it served me well in the end. They were pushing the boundaries, creating a bad omen towards my direction. Hounding me at every resurrection. Stirring the pot brewing for another yearning.

A challenge that had me repeating a mission was disclosing a condition. For the vision had me contaminating the competition, so when I reached my pinnacle, I could hit back. I had to face an interaction from that feast that had me fast forward and press delete.

All while the corrupt return for another feat. Where the only thing that had me facing another inning was the fraction to that friction, that served me a failed mission. Because it was part of a competition that did not meet protocol, it turned he corrupt upside down and inside out.

It left them handling it all with doubt. They got caught red handed creating a war in my peace, trying to Humiliate me with humility, because I stated it first. I had no choice I kept being put in a position worse than I could imagine. They thought they could gang up on me and twist my words around.

Serving me injustice so they can win another inning, had me focused on the corrupts intention and the method moving forward. Because I reached my pinnacle in the middle of a sustainable event it had me facing an incredible interaction where the corrupt saw me as an easy target.

My craft took the initiative and fell into a wrath where no one would dare to compete, compel nor even put me through. The way I got through was unconjurable. It became part of an explainable event that brewing, for the prewarning was only able to be read by those, who were already dead.

They had no life to look ahead, because they were six feet under. Feeding off the rain and the thunder. There was trouble at every blunder, a trap that had me forced to hit back with remorse. I had no choice in the end; I had to state a fact get back on track feed off the impact. I had to create a challenge that served me a willingness to hit back with a tremendous amount of energy. I was to claim the end of that game that served me the force to hit back with remorse. A challenge that served them a will, to return hit back with a brand-new skill.

In the end the only thing that had me face that final inning, was the air that failed me at beginning. It had me face a new improved challenge, that served me well.

It was part of a warning that had me yearning for an upcoming event. It had me stagnant to my development, trying to claim that game.

For every challenge was based on a past trace. A given reason to hit back with treason. For that served trend had me catch up and break the system that led me to fight back an entrance that served me a resurrection to that path that had me regain conscious awareness again.

A willingness to succeed, had me face another thread to that redemption. It had me start again where it had me forced to confide and fall onto the edge of reason so I can remain strong at evert season. I was given the power to override and follow up on an ending that served me well.

A binding spell that became part of a theme, that forced me towards a brand-new scheme. It prevented me from entering a beginning to an end that served me well and forced me to redo reclaim and follow up on another game, hitting a never-ending feast; that broke the silence.

It forced me to release peace. So, when I reached my pinnacle, I could embrace that trace that had me return for another given a challenge. A forbidden key that led me towards a journey that served me a willingness to hit back with sturdiness. In the end the case was erased and the trend.

I was forced to hit back and face another dead end. A

follow up on a trend that had me on the mend. Repeat, regain consciousness and start again; until the end of that trend remained the same, when we meet again. Giving me the reason to undo and face another avenue in the end of that revue.

It had me aim for a better outcome. A challenge that restored my energy and took me on a journey where the corrupt kept feeding off me. I ended up defensive trying to fight off the last cast a spell that had me relapse at the end of that trend that served me a willingness to pretend.

I had to overcome another trace at the end of the race and catch up again. It was warning me I was about to enter a realm that had me retuning for another yearning. For a reoccurring dream became a second coming that is when I knew I hit the end of that review.

It forced me to repeat, repent repel and start from the begging until the end. All while I went through another revelation to a heartfelt destination. I fell in and out of consciousness. A hell forsaken review it had me face another trend all while I hit the end of that final scheme of themes.

A trace that caused an effect led me to a destination where I start again. A trend that served me well in the end. It was to bring me consistent energy because the corrupt kept feeding off me. Creating a war in my peace. Assuming belting me once more will bring me peace.

For they were nowhere to be seen, the road changed the

trace rearranged and the journey remain the same. It served me well every detail had pushed me in the corner and brought me hell just to give in and return for one more heavenly win. Where everything that come from within was a hymn.

Forced to hit back with remorse, once given twice shy third time lucky the third was the lie. Where the breeze, hit the debris it had me face another forthcoming key. Just to cause an effect and feed off the defect. A challenge that had me arrive with intensity, had me silent; divide and conquered.

I was to feed off, ready to release that beast that forced me off the edge humbled. For the energy that served me well, faced me another trap while I went through hell. It took me on a journey to repeat and follow up on a completion lacking vision. For I was to turn in more than one direction.

I had to return face the truth, forced to override a competition. I had to sustain and claim another game. Just to keep up with the program that handed me the evaluation towards a mission that reclaimed a duplicate. A journey that had served its purpose causing the corrupt internal hell.

A repetition had me stepping into the unknown. I was taught a lesson, several ways and every time I hit the end of that drama I would be forced to return and repeat a trace at the end of that forthcoming race. It caused an effect sustainable, ready and willing to face another chilling.

The alarm bells went off, that is when I knew the sweet whispers; were from hungry listeners. Several were undeniable, invalid their approach served me a trace. There was no competition but those who were trying their luck returned hoping they could belt me with bad luck.

It was part of a given to release and follow up on another mission. There were several on my raider forcing me to return and hit back with an expense. I had faced another win; I was taken in it had me repeat another final mission from within. It had me relay a message to finalise that hit with a whim.

It was part of a hint, served a willingness to break that cycle. I was taken for a fool, and for that reason I failed, I got in, had to repeat a test that leaned towards a journey that served me the willingness to hit back with a sly approach. It was part of a trace that had me face a warning.

For every thorough response had me face an entrance. It served me well at the end of that yearning. It was handing me the evaluation to revolutionise that challenge that took its toll. For I needed to reclaim repeat and rebel against those who enter my realm and hit me with an upcoming spell.

I was left to pretend forced to hit back and start again. I was caught up in a web of lies. Several were on my raider serving me with a task that had me revive all while I was trying to survive. I was withstanding leading the pact that had been forthcoming. I was hit with a term to that scheme.

It saved me in between, ready and willing to fight back; God wiling. It had me facing another trace all while the corrupt attempt to trap me at the end of the race. Where every I went had me face another case that was trending at the end of the race and the only witness was that eyewitness.

For the challenge had me hit a final entrance. A task that served me well at the end of that trend. A test that handed me a dead end was forthcoming that is when I knew I hit a raw and created an encore. For corrupt had me foreclose a trial an error and a final vendetta.

It served me well and trapped me when I fell into a given a foundation that served me a tradition. It trapped traced and faced me with a final pushed me in the corner out of hells way so I can return and press replay clearing my name every step of the way.

I had to get back on track, a given theme that had me face another trend in-between. For he who knew caught me in the act of kindness trapping me with a final fact. So, when I reached my pinnacle the only thing that served me well from within was the last thing standing.

For corrupt had me face a yearning there was towards a predicament that had the scheming for another yearning. It had me hit the end of that trend leading me to a destination that was unravelling the corrupts final revelation. The last thing that had me withstanding was the first thing.

I was pushed in the corner, left to repeat a finally. It had me trapped, praised then taken for granted, just to give in and claim another condition from a given momentum from within. just to claim and face another trial and error at every focus. Where every thought served me a willingness to hit back.

I was forced to hit back with a stagnant affair; it brought me forward, hit me with a flare in the air. With a sturdy reminder, and a thorough return, the energy that created the piece had me forced to undo and face a revenue. The journey was earnest; I was stuck once again in the middle of a furnace.

Cold hearted, rock solid ready and willing to push the corrupt in the corner; God willing. The trend was burnt the trace was hit back with a yearning that had me step forward troubling me at every feast all while I walked through that revue face my fear and skip the corrupts method right through.

Forced to return and repeat a trend in the end. It gave me a second chance to sweeten the deal create and create a brand-new ordeal. Then when the pot got hot, I was given an opportunity to hit back with unity. I had to release that beast that served me the everlasting feast.

A curse to that trend had me face a dead-end. Hinting to me the energy that served me well then was the one that took me in and forced me to repeat another warning in the end. I had to enter the trend, cause an effect and press delete. All while I follow up on a key that served me well.

When I face that reality, the dream will conquer all. As I feed off the trace that served me well at the end of that race. It was warning me the only thing that come to be, was the last draw that served me well once more. I was given a reason to hit back with treason; a service well done.

A silent treatment that forced me to release that gave me a second chance to return and face another feast. I was taken for a fool left to repeat and repel against those who forced me to reclaim another division to the game. All while I get in and label the corrupt a rebel from within.

Against the corrupts will, A faith that left them filthy while the rest were hinting to me, I hit a final request. All because the corrupt created a spell, a challenge that handed me an ordeal that served me well. All while I gave in and went through hell. I was to be served well and faced with a vendetta.

When I hit the end, I was failing, for what reason I could not refine. I had come forward and the ideal was a given. It had me face another trace at the end of that trend, where I was haunted by it all. Revealing the one thing that served me well, when I hit that forthcoming enterprise.

The trace was no given the response, was forbidden.

The corrupt hit me with an illicit test, served a unique key, a trace that had me face a new me. Where they banned me, left me final no reserve, no force to hit back no remorse to that cause. Just a dead end hoping I won't make it in the end.

Because I hit the end of that trend, I was taken in it pushed me off the edge straight into a dilemma that had me delayed focused and full of fury. No measure to that pleasure, no trace no ideal ordeal handed me the faith that served me well. I was hindered haunted by the past, living in the present.

I had no freedom no friendship just the energy to create the peace. Even then the trauma handed me the tremor that served me a dilemma. It caused so many interruptions; in the end I fell into a trace that pushed the corrupt in the corner. Faced them with a warning; one that was yearning.

For the corrupts method was ailing, all while they were alienating me. While I hit back and created a better impact, the trace became invalid. It had me replace the old the new and the ending of that trend that had me face an eerie era; where everyone feared me and no one wanted to face me.

All because they served me a trace and I led them on purely to end the race at my pace. That was the only way I could remain strong. All while the rest were ready and willing to belt me God willing. I was on the other end waiting for the corrupt to return and feed off me again.

That is when I knew I was left to feed off that Dealership; that sold me that lemon. For everyone who knew thought cornering me with an everlasting review; will harm me for nothing. What a jinx, I hit the end of that minx coming out the other end facing a tremor and a trial that served me denial.

The undeniable truth led me towards a journey that had me face a case. It was causing an effect and belting me with a defect. The point taken was mistaken, the point given was part of a vision. I was led on and left to repeat face another vision and create a better opposition to that definition.

I hit a connection, linking to he who had me face a resurrection. For he who was creating a war in my peace had me face another feast. It trapped me in the middle of a turning point. I had to fight back face another impact challenge the corrupt at every turning point; just to release and find peace.

For every time I looked within, I found myself hitting an ending that was pending. A trace that had me face another drama at the end of that stigma. It caused an effect and broke the system that served me a willingness to hit back with sturdiness. That journey had me yearning for an enigma.

I fell into a trace that had me face a case. It had me step up a level up, then hit back and face the corrupt. For what I thought was a given had me pretend it was over written. In fact, it was part of a past endeavour that served me well and handed me a vendetta.

For what it was worth, there was no trace nor trend to break the cycle and start again. So, I just kept moving hoping it would all come out soi can continue on my route. because it was a pointless affair And I was handed a trace that served me well it presented with a given precession.

I had to push the corrupt in the corner and sweeten the deal at every final review. It was part of a trial and error and a final vendetta. I was given a theme to break the cycle in-between. So, when I reached that trace the trend will serve me well and break that cycle that put me through hell.

It was part of another trace at the end of the race. It gave me a second chance to return and hit the road. All while the corrupt face a handout to that spread that led me on. It had me work towards a journey that broke the chain cut system and led the corrupt towards a journey of repetition.

It had me forced to repeat another treat. Where every review gave me a silent treatment, it forced me off the edge straight into a pledge. A second coming where I was left to hit of view will hand them a key. It led them towards a journey that served me well at the end of that forthcoming spell.

Because it was part of a given it handed me faith. It was purely to release and follow up another feast. It pushed me off the edge straight into denial. For that method that served me well freed me from that trace; it had me foreclose another case. I was left to face a critical analysis, a test of time.

CHAPTER 7

◆◆◆

When Everything Has A Price Tag

I was on the move, trapped in the middle of a forthcoming riddle. The troubles were refreshed the mess enforced, where I had to catch up and incorporate another compelling force to compress. Face a trace and feed off the mission handing me cause and effect that had defined the drama in the end.

It had me underlined, trapped in the middle of the divine. Where the trace took me in and forced me to reclaim a division from within. It was part of a sacred momentum, a sacrament that had me reach my final redemption to that allegation that served well. Sacrificed at every task handing me venom.

Just to claim a vendetta to a game that served me a validation. It was handing me the next clue. Towards the destination, a task that handed me a retreat to break the chain then claim the game. A gamble forced the corrupt out of that seam that handed them a scheme in-between the theme.

I was finally on the edge on the rough end, ready and willing to start again. Harmed with a lie just to get the truth. In the end I had faced them and hit the trend unravelling that dead end. For the secret was relived, restored recreated and come forth. Lining me up for a key and a test to serve me in time.

What designated was the dream; reincarnated. It served well, presenting me with an upcoming spell. The wish was not part of a trap; it was part of a given momentum to help me get back on track. Torn in more than one direction, handing the corrupt a dead end to that manifestation.

That is when I knew the price off reliving that dream was based on the price that was achievable to the corrupts final. It took me in and had me face another tradition that forced me to hit back with repetition. What took me in took its toll and its time and forced me off the edge.

Trapped in the middle of an upcoming riddle. Just to hit the corrupt with a final indifference. Because they were insensitive to my needs, I was left to repeat repel and follow up on an upcoming spell. The only way they would serve me perse was challenge me with a gift of kindness all the way.

I knew it was not a gift; nothing ever comes good when given. From the start until the end, there is always an obstacle, a challenge that will earn the respect that will serve me an entrance. For the energy that forced me to hit back with a failed debt made me see the whole journey come to be

Where the deck collapses and that dead end traps you in the end. Holding on to that one thing that served me well from within. A given meaning to a lifelong purpose that served me a given caused an effect with an opulence amount of information. That led me towards the next final evaluation.

There is always a face to that trace that will hand you compilation to heave. Every evaluation to that manifestation had me comprehending the truth and confirming the obvious. That was to repeat delete delay and push the corrupt in the corner every step of the way.

The challenges were difficult; I had no idea that the drama was a given. I was left to repeat repel and face another contradiction to that mission. It forced me to complete another competition. All while I was hitting the end of that vision accommodating the end releasing that trend and facing a dead end.

It was forcing me to repeat a dead end, a journey that was a given. It had me face another treason to that mission that served me a purpose at every compelling competition. For the drama was part of a missing link, released, it served me a trend that served its purpose in the end.

It had me face a paradox to that finally, there was a flaw that needed to be dealt with. Warning me there was no trace no trend just a failed attempt to have me reminisce a compelling event. A competition that had me face a tradition, lined me up for another a trial and error a final vendetta.

It had me reserved for an ending, that was pending. A trace that was overpowering, causing effects. Trapped me in the middle of that debt so when I reached my faith in humanity the warning was chaos. The energy that led me to receive, handed me the invasion to complete another plan.

I was yielding for another hold up, creating a war in my piece trying to release peace. All while the rest were on my raider facing a key at the end of that tradition that handed me a final compelling competition. The trend had me repeat a dead end. Waiting for the corrupt to release that beast.

I had to face another feast convince me I was on the road to recovery trying to repeat replace and follow up on another trace a trap that had me face another holdup. For what I thought was the last resort and the beginning of a chaotic event had me face another final trail before I hit denial.

A tradition at the end of that mission, became part of

the road, led towards a recovery. It had me foreclose and face another trace so when I hit the emblem I could violate another presentation to that manifestation. It had me forced to hit back with one more cause of action.

For the journey was part of a curse that served me the willingness to return and come first. I was forced to hit back face another trace and warn the corrupt to stand back and don't count your chicken before they hatch. I was right on track creating an energy that had me forced to hit back.

A final remedy that was up to date, that had me rejoin and create a tradition that served me a well-earned competition. A point taken and one granted was a given and the energy to face another trace at the end of the race was causing an effect and facing me at every defect.

The hate took over, where the journey became open to discussion. It was part of a compelling event that had me face another rude awakening. A final award that had me face another trace was a given reason to hit back with treason. It was part of a tradition that was prewritten.

It gave me a chance to fight back in advance and face a competition. I was rewarded for a key that had me face another rise above that trace. It had me case another given, repeating the same old competition. I was not aware that proposition was part of a trace to stop me from making it happen.

The forbidden clue had me profound and I found myself

fighting for my life outbound. Waiting for the technical issue to fall through, hounding me at every final point of view. With a trace that had me face another feast and a trial that served me the will to return and press delete.

It was only time before I figured out the trace was based on a lie. It had me face a competition. I was served well, left it to the imagination that had me face another compromised situation. Before it came to be, I had the freedom to break the chain that had me face a failed vision.

A tradition at the end of the game, had me face a proposal that was pushing me off my game. It lined me up for one more final release before I fell into pieces. I had to face the fact the corrupt were on my case for all the wrong reasons and the only way I could redo that clue was press replay.

Then try my best to stay away. What a gamble I had to press replay. Because of one mistake I had no freedom to release because the corrupt were on my raider trying to feed off me piece by piece. It put me on the edge of reason where it made me out to be a fabricator to the corrupt final elite.

Waiting for me to fail so they can continue to prevail. It was preparing for the worst curse a challenge that had me reverse. Where the choice was made on a condition, they let it go and allow me to grow. But they had one more plan to complete an ending that had me remove that final dule.

Leaving them unprepared because the journey was too

hard to release. Part of a past test that was parting ways with those who were on my raider trying there hardest to harvest while catching up and facing me at every final incur to that conspiracy. For the truth had me return follow up on a piece.

The turn of events, where my creativity took a turn for a first, an end to that string of events that held me back. Just so I never get back on track, it was handing me the recognition to repeat another vision. For I needed to get back on track and face another trace at the end of the race.

Because I moved on pressed delete, it angered the corrupt. A fierce response that served me a clear path to the next wrath. Because they were on their mission, trying to kick a fuss and break my spirit at every proposal. I was given a trace that had me face a key waiting for me to return; exposed.

The trace that had me replace a trend. A challenge that was warning me I hit a dead end. It left me on relief, for one more case to cease. It was to break the cycle of events, that served me a chance to vent. Before it got worse and the corrupt were returning for one more curse to rehearse.

I took it all in and faced another trace at the end of the race facing another warning to the corrupts serving. Giving me the impression I was lied to by he who saw me as an easy target and assumed making me his victim to his plot will bring him forth and hand me bad thoughts.

For every validation had me face an internal investigation. It had me relist that feast, then repeat another piece, just to release that beast. It had me conform and confront another tornado to that scenario. An event that hit me well and faced me with a given entrance from heaven to hell.

All while I give in and face another evil force from within. The trace at the end of the race, served me a condition that lined me up for another competition. Where every trace was channelling me. Where my existence became the corrupts final resistance. Before they were to return hit with persistence.

A condition that contaminated my mission and force me to return. For I was hit with an expense that rallied up the scores and forced me to hit back with remorse. For every challenge had me face a contradiction to that mission that lined me up for a competition a prize-winning alarming existence.

I found myself in a position worse than I can imagine. Fighting off that demon who returned for another competition. I was led on by those who wanted a piece of the action. Assuming that the mission was forcing me to return for a competition. it was part of a trace that had me face a return.

A turn of events that forced me to rekindle a trace to that mission. Warned me I was not in the right state of mind to claim another division to a game. It forced me to reclaim another test at the end of that progression re-aligning me for a service that had me face another trivial pursuit.

It had me facing a final degree, where I heaved and took it all in independently. I was given the edge of reason followed up on a degree of a bad omen. For what I thought was part of the corrupts trap that had me tricked into thinking I was on the road to repeating.

In fact, I was on the brink of creating a new link. It was part of a path that had me on the edge facing another pledge. Releasing that demon that pushed me forward and faced me with a dead end. All while I tried my best to delete delay and put the corrupt through hell all the way.

I watched them return, while allowing me to release that feast. While they escape holding on to another tape. A trend that had me forced to hit back with remorse, serving me the will to recreate a final force at the end of that cause. Where every abreaction handed me a role to the next encore.

Waiting for me to return for another chase, had me foreclose that risen challenge. A cheap shot at the end of the race. A given opportunity to catch them in act of harming me back-to-back. For the one thing that made me see, was the last thing that stayed within me restoring my energy.

It was the first thing that caused the effects, and the last thing that handed me death threats. That is when I knew I hit a restraint and the corrupt were covering it all up with an intention. I was to blame for everything that went wrong. When was it going to end when they were going to let it go.

I was stuck in a time warp once again fighting a lost cause, so someone else can play my role. If anything, that decision was not my part of that redemption. It was a made-up story by the corrupt to hit me and run, fail me in the long run. No strings attached no follow up to reclaim another game.

I fell into a trace that had me face another given, an informative event that had me repeat replace and create an extension to that redemption. It forced me off the edge repeating another curse. All while the rest belted me with a first and last cover up towards a trace that handed me a follow up.

Where I get in and hit another inning. A thought pattern that haunted me with a false and final replay a rhythm to the beat that helped me get by. Because I fell in the system, I ended up living a nightmare, with daily events and night terrors to add to that failed attempt.

Trying to get out of that system that took me on a path that had me face another vision. A trace ready and willing to repeat and replace, a brand-new creative space. For I was left to decline force my way through so when I caught up, I could repeat catch a break and follow up on another stake.

The one thing that had me face a trace haunted me at

the end of that trend. It handed me devoted declaration, that saw me ready and willing to hit back with a trial and error and a final endeavour. I had to repeat and follow up a trend where corrupt were concocting to break me in the end.

Because my creativity was creating a dead end. A space in-between the old the new and the upcoming review. It became an end of that trend and the beginning of a challenge that had me face another trace. A given reason to replace the old start new and follow up on another review.

Trying not to fall for it was uncanny, because I was caught up in a lie that was harming me to get by. As soon as I was ready to swing from one branch to the next, the corrupt were on the other end repeating and facing me with a trail an error and a final vendetta.

What could I say, the method was dodgy and the corrupt were wasting my time. The lead was a breed, that kept growing, in the end. I gave in I could not fight back anymore. I could not see the point The trace became dramatic the trial systematic. In the end the trace served me well.

It gave me a chance to face my demons in advance. It was the one thing that had me repeat and put me through hell. Warning others that they were right and I was wrong. In the end I gave in, the corrupt were excessively busy, trying to get in and win, leaving me suffering from within.

I could not face another trace, because the corrupt were too busy harming me at every final race. I worked hard to get to where I was, with no recognition no proposition, just a curse that had me rehearse. It was handing me an evaluation to make sure I lose my light at every final destination.

Where every time I hit the end of the race, they took me in faced me from within. It hounded me with a trace that trapped me in the end of the race. They took me in and took me for granted, taking me for a fool and facing me with a free ride from within. Lining me up for another discerning event.

Discriminating me at every turn of events. So, when I reached my peak the only thing withstanding was the drama that had me face another warning. It was forcing me to hit back with a yearning. I never win, because the corrupt saw me as an easy target trying to face me with a follow up.

Years went by and they were still on my raider, trapping me so I never reach my destiny. An expectation that was hard to meet, had become corrupt. The willingness to hit me with a nervous twitch, had me stomped and stagnant beyond my development; trapped leading the wrong pact.

I had to focus, stay simple remain switched on, no allowance to that substance. Because the corrupt were on my raider forcing me to give in. I was on the edge trying to repeat reclaim and face another warning to that game that had yearning for the system to repeat while I repel.

I had to give in, work against the will of those who have been using me to get through. I was left to fight another lost cause, praying to God, they will leave me alone. They were interfering with the mission facing me at every disposal hounding me to do them favours or else hell will break loose.

So, when I reached that trace, it served me well. I was given a reason to break every treason. Where I was on the move, facing another trend. A competition that had me forced to return and pretend. Where I was on the move wasting my time, at the end of the race.

For the composition forced me to return and hit back with a proposal to help me get back on track. I hit a competition and a compelling event that had me forced to fight back and face another trace.
so, when I reached the end of that pinnacle the force hit me with remorse and I remained cynical.

It was the everlasting draw that served me once more and a trace that had me face another given a presentation that served me with a vampire effect that warned me the corrupt were on my raider trapping me at every sample to a simple rule a test of endurance that faced me with an emblem.

It took me by surprise forced me to override and faced me with a warning from within a challenge that will help me endure another review to a system that served me an overview a trace that had me erase a given momentum that lined me up with Delirium.

CHAPTER 8

◆◆◆

A Stagnant Affair Of The Heart

I was causing effects one day at a time, and every step I took, I was taken by surprise. The corrupt had me captured and then returned with an eye for an eye. Ther were trying their best to uncover up another request. The return of a one hit wonder; a rapture like no other.

With the Seventh heaven on the way, I was on the move, trying to attempt to press replay. Where the only eye-witness, that stood its truth, was the hurdle that come my way and protected my spirit every step of the way. For the journey I was chosen to release had me on the edge, pressing delete.

I was on the prowl waiting to be called up but hit a delay, because the corrupt had me face another trace. Traveling from one end to the next heaving at me every step of the way. I was creating a final feast, torn in more than one direction trying to find peace from every resurrection.

The journey that I was handed, was branded, it was part of a play. A fable that was trapping me in the end of that drama that served me a willingness to repeat and start again. If only I knew what was meant to be true, I probably would of gave in earlier and faced another drama.

For the game gave the corrupt a chance to remain idling. I was in the middle of a trap, that became a tradition to hand the corrupt a chance to belt me in advance. The same game but this time around the ending was no longer pending and the trace was a given to repeat repel; against the forbidden.

All so they can catch up feed off my existence, and take whatever was needed. Face another prediction to that mission that served me a wild competition. Where I had to keep my distance, create an expense that served me the will to hit back with a brand-new skill.

For every step I took there was a trace that had me face another cause an effect. It tore me up and had me face another death threat. I was given a momentum to repeat another given so when I reached my peak the end result was forbidden. One thought one trace and then watch it all undo.

It served the corrupt, a chance to fight back, only to witness their plan backfired. They filled their heads with so much redemption it became a debt that warned me I was nowhere near the thread. It became invasive and the trend had forced me to regain another prediction that wailed me down.

What a wrong a move, I had to consume just to claim catch base and follow up on another unwanted claim. It haunted my true existence with a prediction to hand the corrupt a winning streak that failed. I was warned of what was to come from that outcome only to have won, a false predication.

The concept was denied the addiction over written. There was no lead to sacrifice my soul, because the corrupt were on my raider stepping into my dome trying there hardest to convince me I was nowhere near I was meant to be. The troubles were traced the trend replaced, true rude awakening.

The trip down memory lane handed me denial. It was part of a trial that took me in and repeated another repertoire from within. I needed to return and hit the corrupt with a challenge that was conceded. The thought that come my way had me face a trace that was beginning to look interesting.

Stepping forward had me stepping boundaries, landing me in a role where I had to break a rule to get in. Feed off the tradition that handed me a forbidden declaration to that manifestation. It served me a wrongdoing handing the corrupt a chance to repeat repel face me with a forthcoming spell.

All while I was going through hell. That is when I knew the corrupt were on my raider waiting for me to fail all so they can prevail. Attempting to prevent me from living the Holy Grail. I was working towards a direction that had me manifest another resurrection.

The next path to return to break me had me courageous. I was interacting with the wrong, repeating an extension waiting for the corrupt to break me at every sanctum with an inversion. For that invasion was part of the corrupts final indication. Handing me the outlook that served me a willingness to step forward.

It had me facing a trace that had me repeat repel and follow up on another upcoming spell. Where again I was put in a position, that created a challenge that backfired. Leaving the corrupt with a message that served me a trace that had me forced to repeat and hit back with remorse.

Where the upkeep had me repeat an upcoming event. It was denied access handing me the conclusion I was wronged all along by those who were stalking me breeding others to feed off me.
They fell into a trap waiting for me to return and feed off the tradition that served me a well.

The trend had me pretend that the trace was part of a given case. It had me in admin approved while I improvised and followed up on a trend that had me forced to protect myself while that trace put me through hell. It served me a willingness to reveal what I thought will bring forth peace.

But all it did was release the beast and test the patience of those who feast. Then have to give in because I found myself in a position attracting the wrong. I had to repeat claim and follow up on another game. Trapping those who remain the same and vigilant to the game.

A trace that caused an effect, broke the system. It took me on a journey that led me astray. Focusing on what was real had me face another trace causing the wrong effects. Because the lie took over the truth, I was given a reason to repeat and reclaim another vision to the mission.

The only way out, was create a war, in he who returned to belt me once more. A failed attempt to return, press replay a given opposition to repeat and press delete. I had to reclaim a command to that brand a proposition that served me an alliance. It broke that chain in the corrupts domain.

It had me brave once again, for that momentum had changed, it had me sprain that train of thought. For that gamble that was to be played in my head, remained idling, until they found a way out. I had to reverse that curse, that simultaneously took its first step, into my existence.

What a vision I had to overcome just to repeat an outcome. For the case was overwritten the trend had me face an enigma to that challenge that served me a vision. It was overpowering my mission. I had to reclaim follow upon another outcome. Facing a dead end and a death threat in the end.

For every step I took served me the ending that was pending. It was creating an entrance that was never ending. It handed me a dead end at the end of that trend. It gave me a second chance to dive into a trace, that served me a willingness to end that trend that warned me I hit a dead end.

The race had given me the faith to return for one more key. The sooner I got through, the later it took me to face another final review. It weas part of a given trapping those who knew in the corner so I can get in and conquer another trace to get in and face another inning.

It had me forced to hit back with remorse and challenge the corrupt at the end of that cause of action. I was meant to repeat face another feat, create a presentation that had me forced to hit back with an allegation. It made me meet my maker sooner than later preparing me for my rights.

What a day to remember a memory I wish to forget. For the reason being I was to clear my name again, by those who were bred to face feed and leave me stagnant to my development. Several found an opportunity to cover up everything, by pushing me in the corner and driving me insane.

I was hanging from a thread waiting to reach my pinnacle and start again. For my hard had paid off but my potential took me on another roller coaster ride. I was given another hit by those who were ready and willing to praise me to my face but cut my skin my cords and leave me God willing.

In the end I gave in fighting a lost cause even though I was in. They needed me too to get through too. I was not ging to give them a chance to repeat another theme hoping I would fall for the same goal. The one that was certain I was in it to waste another trace hitting me at the end of the race.

My instincts kicked in my trace handed me an evaluation to break the trace and force the corrupt out of the equation. In hindsight the road they chose was to harm me at my best stepping into my domain as if I was part of their conquest. The fact I had no intention of returning for a redemption.

It served me a presentation that led me towards a journey where the corrupt turned. All because they owed me a dime a dozen, a challenge that had me face another interaction towards a reservation. It stirred the pot and forced me to hit back with one more cause and effect.

A trace to help me resurrect and face another feast became apparent. Because the corrupt had me as an opponent it forced me to hit back like I had no faith. Instead of paying me what they owe me they went off the rails serving me a sentence instead of handing me a valued response.

A warm welcome was all I wanted, but the corrupt

turned cold while they turned little dirty tricks into dirty little secrets. Judged me as if they were better and I was less likely to survive that dive. The fact I was chosen to raise awareness did not raise an eyebrow.

It was as if I had to play the part and put up with the drama that followed. It had got to the point I had no frail path left, to deny what I had. For in the end of the road the beginning led me towards a journey that will hand me dead-end; no given a chance to rise above that praise.

Where that rude awakening, became second best. A chance, to challenge to rise above and beyond the rest. For what I thought will keep me strong and occupied, actually broke the chain reaction. It pushed the corrupt off the raider straight into a delay that handed them denial all the way.
It was part of an infectious dilemma delayed, stating facts. It had me causing effects, just to hit back with remorse. It was following up on a given. A track record that handed me troubles. It stated facts while pending, just to get back on track. Served well and forced to return for one more turn.

The journey that raised hell took me on a path that served me well. I was on hold trying my hardest to dissolve. For the trace was a given to break in-between. Where I hit back with an upcoming spell. A given chance to hand me the results to face another trace. Then give in at the end of the race.

I needed to return and face a given, a chance to advance

resurrect and face another trace at the end of the race. A tradition that handed me failure first. A composition, that caused an effect, it had me face another trace at the end of that trend. It served me the willingness to look forward not back.

A faith less likely for me to fail, became second best to that final test. Because the corrupt were ready willing and able, it had me stepping into the unbreakable event. The journey had me face a one hit wonder, it had me wasting credit, unravelling the old starting fresh and creating a trace.

It had me foreclose a case that was weighing me down. A challenge that had me forced, to hit back with remorse. The warnings were unprecedented, that thought was uncanny, praising the wrong, because it was the wrong who remained strong. In the end, the energy that stated it also created it.

It had me forced to hit back and break the trend all while I got in and faced another inning from within. There was trouble in the mist a case that had me hit back with a twist. It was part of unstable label challenging me at every fable event. I was chosen to create a piece and face another feast.

For the corrupt saw me as an easy target trying to find peace. They were relying on me to get by. For they knew where I was heading and who was reaching their everlasting setting. It served me a holdup it gave me a chance to fight back in advance; there was no faith no trace to replace.

No chance in hell of repeating that spell, for the corrupt had to fight back. Facing me with a challenge to get me back on track. Forced to hit back with remorse, was breaking the silence so the corrupt come forth. A journey that was put on hold, for the dates had changed the challenges rearranged.

That is when I knew I hit a review, the hard truth that could not be sustained. The corrupt were willing and able to hit me run with no clue to justify their outcome. I was searching for facts but all I got was a dead end in the end handing the corrupt a chance to face me in advance.

I had to remain vigilant to a game that had me forced to hit back with remorse. A challenge that had me overcome an interlude in the long run. That is when I knew I hit the end of that trend that caused an effect and created a piece that served me well at the end of that spell.

They were returning to press replay a final vendetta, served like no other. Only to witness I hit an eyewitness, leading him to a destination where their journey hit the end of that reification. It was serving me a destination, well worth the wait. Leaving me suffering in silence while the rest defiant.

Waiting for the next king hit, at the end of that request was serving me, conscious awareness. For the result I need to accommodate, had me remain silent. While the rest violate and then sustain another trend at the end of the game. A follow up on a rise above all; an occasion that had me saved.

Served an ending to break the cycle in advance. I was true to myself that word had me face another reality kick. a trace that served me the indifference handing me the choice that had me rejoice. It had me fighting for my life double time. I had to fake it all just to find solace from that fall.

It forced me off the edge, pushed me in the corner straight into a ditch. Here I was again starting a new phase, an era that had me force that closure that served me a willingness to hit back with sturdiness. Where the corrupt had me face them and hit me with a traumatic event.

Where this time around, I was praising no one of importance. I hit a downside and presented those who knew with a full-blown clue. Out of mind, out of sight a task that served me wrong and served the corrupt right. What they assumed was not true, was part of a curse that had come first.

I was about to come forth and reverse, to that everlasting curse, facing them with a reality check. Circulating from one end to the next handling that trace with no care in the world. That is what had me face another rapture so when I caught up and hit a rapture. A task that hit the final escape.

The corrupt had no chance in hell of completing that task. Time did not standstill and I was on the edge holding on to what I believed was my path in fact it was part of a trace that led me to repeat repel and follow up on another forthcoming spell. I fell into a trap that had me embrace that event.

It saw me through it had me face another given just to break the system and fail the mission. I was torn in more than direction; it saw me forced to hit back with what I thought was the last resort. Introducing the corrupt towards a lead the last reveal before I hit a new skill.

It had me forced to hit back with remorse. I continued to rebel against those who were story telling. The trend was no cause for alarm, but then again, action was needed. Because the corrupt saw me feeding off the trend creating a Dynasty that served me a willingness to study that sturdy haul.

A hold up, with a pull back, to push me off the edge and straight off track. Wasa begging to look extremely overwhelming. I had to face a trace a given reason to follow up on a treason. With an added response. I had to hit back out of spite trying to face a trace at the end of the race.

It forced to hit back with remorse; I gave it my best shot and realized the only thing that was standing was enduring and I barely survived. Leading me towards a direction that was unravelling. Facing me with a clue that had me forced to hit back with a review. A task that took me in failed me periodically.

Where I had to refine and follow up on another key. A day where I had to face my truth, for reality had me on the brink stepping into the unknown. It had me waiting patiently to repeat and repel against that forthcoming spell. A presentation that had me fast-forward and pressing replay.

It was causing effects, warned of what was to come from that outcome. Waiting for the truth to set me free, a lead towards a destination that warned me I had no freedom nor foundation to step up forming a reserve. It was just a follow up to set me up for a fall, all while I return and rise above it all.

It locked me in a world where the corrupt had me on the brink of a breakdown. Apparently, I owed them a favour, they returned to hit back with a safety net at the end of that trend. It forced me to repeat and repel against that demon from hell. Breaking that cycle that put me through hell.

I was torn, in more than one direction, they had me under the raider lining me up for another cover up. An attempt to throw away the key that I earned periodically. Assuming that method will fix everything from within. In fact, it taught me a valuable lesson never to tread, on an inquisition.

CHAPTER 9

◆ ◆ ◆

A Devine Calling

Forced to face another waste, a given momentum to release that Demon from that case. I was handed a test to delete delay and take advantage of the corrupts mission all the way. It was harming me, unnoticed and I at every forthcoming clue had me face another final review.

With an incantation to that manifestation, and a follow up to the next destination. There was a competition that had me face another proposition. I was to re-examine that famine and follow up on another contradiction to that mission, before I made my decision.

It forced me to repeat, repel against those who knew. Faced with a challenge from within, all so they can get through. I was served a well-deserved vision, a desire to that mission that had me forced to hit back with a validation. It had me sense I hit the end of that trend with a warning.

It had me on the edge where the corrupt were on a mission. They were about to kick me in the curb because they hit a reserve. Because I fell into a tradition, with a final recreation to that manifestation it had me facing the end of that trend with a well-deserved meaning in the end.

I was served well at every mission the test took its toll, and I fell into another hell raising hole.
It had me face another forthcoming event, the one that had me forced to sit back with a final interlude. I was to face another trace a given thought that served me the reason to return.

I had to face a trace, where every trend led me to break the system. I had to recreate another cozy affair, a challenge that brought me forward, not only they had me as bait, but they haunted me with clickbait. That is when I knew I hit the end trying my luck to force me to hit back with bad luck.

It had me click and collect all while the rest get in and repeat repel and face another forthcoming spell. Rejected for using me to get through had me in dire straits. Standing strong praising the wrong and when the time come break the cycle and remain vigilant while I start all over again.

I was on the move but there was several working with the system pushing me off the edge, so I never get in or pledge from within. That is when I knew I hit a constant reminder the troubled doubled and the trace became part of a case that forced me to hit back with a curse I could not reverse.

I had no choice there were several on my raider forcing me to hit back. For my comfort was hit and the corrupt a challenge that warned me there was no trace no trend no challenge to belt me in the end. Just a final feast to re-claim and follow up on brand new train of thought.

A trace that forced me off the bend, lined me up for one more chance to release that beast. I had to repeat another trace at the end of the race. Then repel against those who put me through hell. Warned what was to come from that outcome. It had me second guessing and starting again.

They were trapping me trying to get me to pitch in. Only to witness they hit me with a first and last curse. They were causing effects and courageously pushing me off the edge. For those who were reminiscing just to reclaim the game were taken for granted, for it was a gamble taken foolishly.

I had to restart, create a task at the ended that trend just before I hit a dead end. It forced me to break the cycle and pretend that the journey was too hard to repeat. It had me facing a warning, a knowing that the outcome was forthcoming and the challenge was way over the top.

It had got to the point, the corrupt were on my raider. Purely to remind me one false move and I will not see the light nor a bright future ahead of me. It got to the point I gave in, obviously my journey was harming those who knew and could not wait to reclaim another division to the game.

For their existence had value and mine was just part of a bad day on their end perse. Where I could not return nor desire or deserve another empire. My patience ran thin and all in all I fell into a bed win. Where that trap had me unprecedented, I did not deserve to play nor press replay.

I was stuck praying for God to guide me through, out of that dark hole. For it had me regret ever stepping into a realm that served me wrong, it had me strong, off the rail in the long haul. Where in the end I hit a dead end facing a contraption that had me forced to hit back with redemption.

The journey I chose was an easy task. I was stuck trapped in the middle of that trend preparing myself for another dead end. For what I assumed and what was to come from that outcome became part of a journey that led me towards the end of a dream. It had me redeem another scheme.

The journey was too hard to embrace; I lost that lust and the passion to help me robust. It had me face another hustle. About to be pushed towards a direction with no entrance to that dream that harmed me in-between. To many hold up no loophole just a conspiracy to lead me to destruction.

It took me down, all so I give in and ignore the fact I had no challenge to push me off track. It had me face another trace from within. Where I no longer have part of the review. It had me focused with one thought and hit with the last resort. Face a final case a given to return for one more misfortune.

A trip down memory lane, had me reminiscing the end of that tradition. I had one more chance to hit back with repetition, only to witness I hit a deposition. It took me on a journey that led me towards a final provision to that admiration that took over and handed me a brand-new evaluation.

A failed proposal turned the corrupt upside-down. They led me towards a journey where my raider waiting for the pin to drop so they can prevail and I fail and rot. For the corrupts journey had me yearning for one more clue. It took me in and ran its cause an action that handed me an abreaction.

They were hoping I lose hope and a follow up towards a path of harmful addictions. For that was the motive of several who lost their lives for no apparent reason. The journey I was on became a harmful prediction. If I did not tread carefully the path I was on will turn against me for way too long.

That thought wave, hit the corrupt with a heat wave. It served them the wrong start a given permission to create a fresh start. A challenge that will serve them well, forced me to catch up early and create another follow up to a journey that lined me up for a key that turned me.

Enforced to hit back with one more chance to get back on track. Beat the corrupt to the punch, it handed me a hunch, that served me a predicament that poisoned my spirit. Now my head was stuck fighting off another demon that had me forced to hit back for no reason.

I was forced off the edge straight into conviction that handed me a brand-new competition. What a trust that handed me the last laugh. I had carried it towards the next path where in the end of that trend it served me a challenge that serve me a brand new beginning a chance to hit back in advance.

That forceful event saw me as an easy target. For that reason, I continued running on the hope I beat the buzzer and the corrupt to the punch and hand them a failed hunch. For I knew I was being watched by those who could not wait to see me fail so I never prevail.

But all it did was lead me towards the wrong path. Proving I was innocent made the corrupt Milicent. An extension to that redemption that forced me to revive another serenity to that melody. An ending that race with ease to that cease. for the next creative sense was too hard to restore.

I realized too little too late that the dream was being tarnished in-between. I lost the drive and the reason to catch up, because the corrupt saw me easy they were on my case turning tricks. Feeding other lies, waiting for me to fail so they can return for another hit.

This time around I saw the light took it all in, waiting for what I thought was the last resort. I fought back from within, for what good did it do, only time will tell all I knew I hit a trace that served me well and forced me to hit back while I heaved at every seam fell into to a heap breaking the chain.

I prayed at every whim I win and lead the corrupt to a destination where they no longer see the light or even take a minute to fight. For that reason, I hit justice a forbidden fight. Giving me the opportunity to stand tall and not allow the corrupt to enter my realm and face me.

For they were returning to steal for one more crown. Then erase that trace forcing me to give in and reveal another win, to that destruction that solved the riddle from within. In the end the journey that seemed too hard to conquer, was just part of a trend that had me hit a hold up in the end.

A service that saw me fall out of place a place. It took me in and presented me with a brand-new key a challenge that had me see I was nowhere near I was to be. It was easier to pretend so I can give in and start again. I gave in and presented the corrupt with one more reason to win.

I was to face a trace and prepare myself for one more key. A chance, to hit back in advance.
A reality kick that took over and sent the corrupt packing. Leading them to a destination where they lose reservation. A chance to hit back in advance, had me face a trick and trip down memory lane.

The door shut, completely and left me profound and let down. Assuming attempting to steal another key from me will hand them a first, foremost, a brand-new priority. It was proven that journey was a hoax to hand me a challenge where in the end I had no freedom nor foundation to pretend.

It had me reliving a nightmare and in denial. Where I continued on my path holding on to a score that had me face an encore. I had more key to earn but that breed who knew could not wait to return and feed off me periodically. A theme and a given reason to hit back with treason.

Where that constant reminder had me facing another trial and error. Pretending that the journey was pending and the given key was never ending. The trend had me hit a dead end a final vendetta to serve me well in the end of that burden that put me through hell.

I was taken for a fool, left to produce another review. Just to get back on track and create a customary attack. It was forcing me to hit back with redemption, towards a manifestation. That lined me up for a final. An indication I hit a final arrangement, trapped in the middle of a presentation.

Reaping a reward at every destination, was making the corrupt feel uneasy, trying their luck to face me with a bad omen, where everything I did to break the chain had me face a tradition that was forcing me to repeat a composition. It had them facing a crisis, that pushed them in the corner.

It drove them absolutely insane, how far I came. They were sworn to secrecy, drawn to me with envy. Assuming that the energy that served me was the energy I was to share with those who were aware. I was too free them from that force that handed them remorse create a junction of redemption.

Where every thought taught them a lesson, handing m evaluation to embrace another trace. Warning me the only thing that had me standing with rhythm was the trial the error and the final vendetta. All while trying to trap me and interrogate me once again.

For what I thought was a given, gift had me on the edge revising another pledge. It forced to hit back with remorse creating an encore to that uproar. It had rally, move on relying on nobody to remain strong. Because the road I was on had me face another trace.

Serving me a foundation to complete and comply remain the same and get by. Just to repeat a competition that had me on a mission, protecting me at every voyage. A follow up on another red flag, that swore I was branded by those who were scheming to scam me at every release.

I was surrounded by several who knew me and wanted to screw me. Embracing what I knew and engaging in a séance handing me a scene from a horror movie. I had many on my raider gaining wisdom acclaiming a trace at the end of that trilogy; that served me a lack of unity.

I had to reclaim and follow up on another given. A trace that handed me a torch lit to hit back with no regret. Because I was hit way before I had a chance to relight another flame. The corrupt were on my raider retaliating and I on the other end protecting myself from a thread.

I had no idea I was hitting a dead end at the end of that trend. For what I assumed was part of a condition was meant to help me move forward with the indication I hit a destruction with no discretion. It had me restoring someone else's energy stepping into the unknown.

Where the corrupt became territorial, leading me towards a direction that messed up my head. They were throwing me a bone and leaving me alone while I'm chewing and brewing on it. Meanwhile continue to come up with ways to harm me from within. With no such luck to begin a new inning.

The journey was way too harsh to overcome. Because there were to many on my raider, waiting for me to give in and fail me at every degree because they envied me. It was not an envy of pure jealousy it was a malicious vicious conspiracy to stop me from living my destiny.

They were handing me an energy that served me the willingness to escape unharmed, because they saw me easy. They were raising an alarm hoping I would have no problem returning the favour.

There was a dilemma that had me delaying every trial and error. The journey I chose had the corrupt dead to the bone. Warning others to back off for they were about to get jerked off. There dirty trick of returning to harm me with a yearning backfired. They were instigating a fight recreating a tremor.

With an invasion to that instigation there was a trace that had me face another interrogation that lined me up for one more review it served me well and presented the corrupt with one more upcoming spell. It had me regain and reclaim another delay to that insightful vendetta.

Where I hit a hold up and repeated a challenge that warned me. There was no trouble, trace nor a trend or tremor to replace. The corrupt were excessively busy living in the past. Collecting Data and waiting for me to break, so they can continue to repeat. A follow up on another trick to the trade.

It had me regaining conscious awareness from that wake. I was nowhere near that catastrophe. I was harmed, to the core my spirit hit an encore that is when I knew I had to repeat and follow up on another review. They had me surrendering way too early for I had no reason to hit back with treason.

It was the only way I could return and state a fact. Follow up on a tradition that had me hitting a final repetition. Forced me off the edge warned of that proposal a preach that had me pledge. It gave me a second chance to hit back in advance preparing myself for more day to step into another replay.

I was on the move, each day had a counterplay. Each momentum had a vampire effect; time did not stand still it had me face another given. A challenge that warned me I hit the end of that tradition, forced me off the edge. Trapping the corrupt in the middle of a forthcoming riddle.

For me to get back on track had me face another final impact. I was taught a lesson once again looking as if I was to blame while the corrupt tortured and hit me intentionally in my domain. They took me in and broke my faith in humanity and the system once again.

Waiting patiently had me living on the edge. Reliving a n nightmare fighting a lost cause creating a challenge that had me face a true reality. Wasting valuable time reminiscing the old, because I lost the meaning to that dream that served me wonders in-between.

I was robust, full of energy no time to release that demonic feast. The corrupt saw it as a threat, they had me locked in waiting for me to face another trace creating my eulogy before I had a chance to prove my innocence in advance. I was as an easy target; they forced me in haunting me from within.

Cornered by the lie, pushed me beyond repair. Lining me up to sin, so they can create a barrier from within. The burial ground before my time was leaving me suffering in silence so they can deny me access and create a challenge that had me forced to hit back with remorse.

They were waiting for me to fail so they can prevail. All for one and one for all, a feast that served me a relief and challenge that had me face a return. Warning me I hit a wrong turn then a home run making sure next time they enter my realm they will seal the deal and serve me a rude awakening.

I was lost for words on the move, warned of what was to come from that final outcome. It had me on the other end forming a new trace and a trend that caused an effect and shook me, so I never resurrect. I was to lose and the corrupt win a vision from that final arrangement leaving me stern.

CHAPTER 10

◆◆◆

When A Trap Becomes Obsolete

A unique, challenge forced me to delay and press delete. Warned of the intention, once again, it lined up for redemption so the corrupt can return for another chance to face me and fail me in advance. Preparing me for a competition that was pre-existent. There was pardon to that post.

It was the corrupts way of entering my realm and pressing replay. Assuming they won everything, after the fact for hitting me and running continuously, put them back on track. The last hit harmed me mentally physically but not spiritually. This time around the spirit stood his ground.

My spirit stepped in, broke the corrupts mission, clouding their vision from within. They were trapped, in a time warp, starting a fight, making sure they turn against me. It was only the way they could give in win a fight and regret ever entering my realm because I was already in profound.

Despising them from within, wishing them hell at every whim. It was my way of accepting the fact they were on my raider wishing me the same luck. They made me sick with worry, not only was I entertained by the entrance, but what I had to experience was absolutely terrifying.

The path I was on was out of character for me. Not only I was left to repeat but the corrupt were summoning me to press delete. It turned me upside down because what I was chosen to do was being tarnished by those who knew. They wanted to hit me and run and screw me right through.

I was stuck in a rut, streaming and skipping everything to remain strong. Trying to come to terms with the fact the corrupt were troubling me on purpose; just to get back on track. It forced me to fight back I was so delusional because of the corrupts method. it had me fighting a lost cause again.

All because they were on my raider trying to harm me again with the same game. Leading me towards a destination where I gamble my life away. Lucky for me I had my spirit by my side warning me the corrupt were wearing a weapon of destruction; hoping I fell for the next lie.

I was forced to look within, face a challenge and the corrupts system from within. All so they never get in with the same detection from within. For this time around I played it purely to catch them in the act of harming me. For what they thought was a given was test and they failed it immensely.

Because of it, they became hostile, the more they pushed the less likely I gave in. It got to the point they read my story plot and decided to use it as a weapon to harm me and my dignity. To my defence I wrote it to see who was watching me and caught the culprit and corrupt red handed.

Now I was torn paying for what I thought was the last resort. Where was my spirit, when I needed to repeat and reclaim another trace at the end of that forthcoming case. I was led on left to repeat so when I caught up, I could press delete. In the end what can I say I was back to where I started.
I was no better off than before, nowhere near the worst either. I had to many hang ups, way too many flaws. I was given a thorough reason and a response to reclaim another division to the game. I had to acclaim that faith that warned me I was about to hit a home run.

Forcing me to repeat repel and give in, in the long run. For the corrupt had it in for me from the beginning. I hit another chance to advance and a trend to repeat a revealing. A meeting where the corrupt met up and forced me to hit back waiting for me to fail so they can prevail.

I had to disembark and reclaim a follow up to the game. It was presenting me with a force to prepare me for one more key. It had me return the favour and reclaim one more chance to embrace that trace. For waiting for the corrupt to return and reclaim another direction to a game had me proper.

I was grounded, challenging myself at every trend. Waiting for the corrupt to return and belt me again. where the world I once knew created a piece it forced to return and hit back with an encore at the end of that release. I was taken for a fool and left to repeat and follow up on another given.

Feeding of the concept while the rest took on an oath, it forced me to hit back with a final wrap. I was debating while the corrupt were deleting, they had me questioning everything. Where each method had me declining that role and each trend had me on the edge of reason. First and last.

It had me facing an accountable force to hit back and repeat a trial. For that error at the end of that vendetta became really interesting. The wall climbing up to catch up was corrupt, I was not aware I was being groomed, purely to face my true destiny, at the end of the race.

It had me relay messages so when I reach the point of no return; the gamble was no given. For the great wall collapsed, was Leading the corrupt towards a dead end a destination where there was no value to society views nor was there a moment for me to break the system, feeding off the mission.

I had them fighting a lost cause, an ending that was spending handing me the ease from the trace that took me in and forced me to replace another trauma from within. Waiting patiently to reap a reward mind boggling I was working all hours on the clock no recognition just a failed proposition.

I had faced with a given, a reminder I hit a failed competition. All so the corrupt prepare me for a trial an error and an attempt to hand me terror. Then when the time come and I knew I was ready and willing to prepare me for another vendetta after I hit the end of the tremor.

I no longer wished to get involved, in their little games. The benevolent effect was fake false and misleading. It was a prediction to hand me an evaluation to restore my energy and feed off the investigation. I created a piece to piece together a new improved feast.

It was part of a phase, a trace that took me on a journey, with a revelation. I was left to release that beast that took me for granted. I was faced with an ending that had me forced to work on what I thought was a challenge. The corrupt stated a reason and repeated it by attempted to replace me.

I was not prepared for that trace; others had their way because they were planning to hit me every step of the way. For resolution to that method was one sided. It was over before it began and I hit a hold up, so I never reach that peak that had me on the run ready to resolve the outcome.

The challenge I was handed was a part of a preach, it landed me in role that had me branded. All so I had to return for another chance to belt the corrupt in advance. In fact, all it did was release that beast that had me facing another interrogation. taken for granted by those who knew.
Leaving me infectious, leading me to a destination where every challenge had me face contagious investigation. They were ganging up on me. Purely to harm me before I had a chance to face another trace in advance. For those who had a clue, were debating how to enter my realm and feed off me.

Repeat, whatever they did when I least had expected it. Then take me as a fool and delete it. For the given response had me face a trace and break me instantaneously. Just so I can force their way in. Waiting for them to return and conspire with whomever just to repeat and reclaim a diversion.

For the game had me face a case and conspire with whomever to trouble me like no other. For corrupt had to dive into a trace had me face another window to opportunity. I had to face that lead, then disclose that treachery unbroken being caught. That secret enemy had other intentions.

He bred others to undo and overpower me right through. I was torn in more than one direction. Just to reclaim another thought, hounding me at that given time. He who was on the move had me reclaim a final, a declined tack to that manifestation handing me the evaluation.

I had to heave at he who harmed me. For he had other intentions and the only way I could undo and face another review was catch up; break the cycle. Before the corrupt returned and hit me at arrival. For that generation gap to the game was unreasonable. A fine line between the lie and the truth.

A ride to justify the action of he who had me repeat another abreaction. A presentation that was trending had me facing another trial that was never ending. It was a hit and run hitting me with denial, so the corrupt can challenge me feeding off the trend that stood time.

It was part of an entrance to break me with a vengeance. All it did was oust them out hand them doubt and another wide world catastrophe. The journey I was on was denied by those who wished to see me six feet under. Instead of favouring me like it was meant to be before I hit down under.

The opposite effect had come and gone. For what I assumed occurred was all in the air. For what I knew was just a failed review. For the last time, the lost haul, brought home hope, and the fall from Faith. Where it all turned grey and everything surrounding me got interesting.

The corrupt got caught up in greed a financial lead. Just

to bring forth a road not worth justifying.
I felt the passion the curse, reverse and all of the drama endure while the rest face another test. Giving me the permission to embrace another mission to that composition.

I had to engrave that trend that served me a well. Align me with a vendetta in the end. Where this time around, I'm back to front, left to right, forced to hit back ready to fight. Only to see the corrupt were prompt on my raider warning me to see what was really happening to me.

For their fear kicked in, it was pretty obvious; purely to challenge me with a feast from within.
For the trend had me face a dead end and a challenge served me well. In the end they entered at the own risk failing every trace and trip down memory lane waiting for me to fail so they can prevail.

He who gained knowledge, to restore his energy, by feeding off me; had become entertainment. I had no freedom to repeat a sanctum. Because I was stuck in the middle of an odd moment trying to come to terms with the fact I was pushed off the edge trying to get back on track.

For the first time was harmful, the second was destructive the third was productive. By the time I hit the fourth and final recall, I had to return for the last time. T claim another indifference and feed off the trace that was leading me to a traditional case. On the other end, warning me once again.
I was no further out of the woods than I was supposed

to be. I was not aware my light was being dimmed by the corrupts final whim. What I assumed had me face another trace, created a war in my peace. There was too much to do and no back up to reclaim redo and follow up on another review.

The corrupt were on my raider, trying to release that beast. I had to fight back and find peace. Because the corrupt saw me as easy target, the same contest to that conquest became a dead end to that quest. Where the journey was cut short and the dream hit me with the last resort.

For they all hit back with trace, it kept circulating keeping me occupied. All so I never reach my potential. Where I had to face another final trend in the end. The challenge had depleted the plot deleted. The freedom was cut short no foundation to release that feast; a purpose well served.

It was part of evolution to break the corrupts restitution. An evaluation to amend that everlasting trend. Praised me while I hit the end of that manifestation the restored whatever energy I had left because the drama had become quite complexed and I hit the end of that trend returning the favour.

It comes to my attention the corrupt had a final, and each redemption, gave me a chance to follow up on a trace that served me well at the end of that forthcoming spell. It caused an effect and created a feast where each outcome took me in and attempted to my spirit from within.

Assuming that will serve them well from within. Lucky for me my spirit is not only the leader of the pact, but it is the one who created the piece. Bring forth peace love and life back to the soul where humanity needs to look from within create war in peace; an outcome that will help in the long run.

I had to look from within, trace that trap that served me a willingness to get in and win. I had to return and face what I thought was the end of that dead end. It had me forced to hit back with remorse. Combine combust bring forth peace, so when I caught up, I could heave at the corrupt.

I had to follow up on another feast just to claim, catch up and remain servant to the game. My vision became part of my intuition and the lack of case that served me a feast. This time around they did not let me down not gently but violently. It led me to towards a journey that had me find peace.

My intuition served me well, the realization to that manifestation was part of a competition. It had me forced to hit back with repetition. That is when I knew I hit the end of that trend. It took me in and had me start fresh again. There was no task worth the troubles nor a treatment to follow up on.

Only a case to that method that had me forced to repeat replace and cover up another trace. Giving me the permission to break the corrupts mission entirely. Leaving them suffering in silence because the method was undone one-sided heaving at me at every outcome.

from that cause of action was just a trace to hand me a curse. I had to revive and follow upon another verse. Because I dived into the unknown hoping this time, I could return repeat and force the corrupt to press delete. They were on my raider, hoping I had given in and hand them a win.

This time around I played it, completed my task and followed it through. On a journey that had me face a trail error and a tradition that will feed off the mission. Handing the corrupt a dead end to that competition. If anyone was to return to click and collect it would be me because I fell into a key.

For they enforced their way in, fed off my energy from within. They played me like a fiddle peaked at every riddle. I was left to hit back with a challenge that had me get back on track, fighting a lost cause. The game had me infused with false and fake friendships; used as clickbait.

Leading me to a destination that had me face another awakening. They would click their fingers and I obedient as I would play it, to keep the peace; have everything remain the same. Because I was on a mission to complete my tasks, others saw it as a threat to break the chain.

They took me in and belted me at the end of that trend from within. My health deteriorated I could not understand why. I was healthy kept fit even ate the right foods to keep me from losing my way. But I bought a beverage from an entity that was conspiring with others to harm me.

In the end they took me in and broke me physically from within. My spirit took over forced me to fight back. The poison took me on a path of a relentless task the stress took its toll, literally pushed me straight onto the pay role. It had me face a driven, a momentum that served me a sanctum.

It had me pass another test; it took me on a journey that had me rise above the rest. It made the unethical, more anxious, angrier than before, the more they hit the less they achieved. The assumption became redemption. I had no freedom to delay for the corrupt handed me decay.

I had to declare and face another trace. Follow up on a case that had me replaced. It took me on journey where I was given a reason to repeat, repel and follow up on another given. Where this time around I forced my way in broke the system and gave them something to truly think about.

A trend to hand the corrupt a true rude awakening in the end. For they knew where to hit where to run and what buttons to press. Because they had an insider harming me with a final request. instead of helping me get through the way it was stated they used abused led me on and left me rebuked.

I was pushed in the corner so I can remain strong. I had

one more chance to repeat, rebel and repel against those who were conspiring to harm me behind the scenes. I caught them in the act of extending that drama. Instead of me looking bright, they twisted my words around, serving me right.

The trace was a case that had been given a name. A train of thought to reclaim a definition to that vision. It was hinting to the corrupt, that I had more than one chance, to catch them in the act of serving me a bad omen. It made them worse, causing an effect creating the wrong cause of action.

They had me tickled pink, on an expense that was about to cost me my life. It had me outline it all to my favour; then think quick. I knew whatever I did my journey will slumber and I will find myself hitting thunder. They had more manpower than I, they had income and fed many with plenty.

They would recruit another troop, to have me surrender my liability. Leaving suffering in silence while the rest face another trace terribly laughing at me as if their trend forced me to return and break the silence again. Hinting to me I was to blame for the world hitting catastrophe.

Just to cover up the lie and then return to harm me from within. They were hitting on a daily dose where every time I sweetened the deal the journey became way too hard to deal with because I had a little mouth to feed the burden of trying to keep myself alive added another little life on my side.

Leaving me on my own waiting for them to return and hit me once again. With a trial an error and a trace that had me face another tremor. Where this time around; they troubled me on a different level. What was said was not true and instead of marking it as a lie. They instigated a fight to get in.

It created a war in my peace and forced me to fake my death on the hope I resurrect. Look forward not back and regret ever stating a new fact. Every momentum had me facing another informative evaluation from that manipulation. Everything from the beginning changed, I lost a reservation.

I had no foundation nor freedom to decline; I could not override or even subside. I had restrictions towards a method that was meant for me to rise not depreciate while the take me for granted and leave me branded. For those who knew could not stand the fact I was chosen.

They wanted to push me off track, they tested my patience and had me forced to hit back with a vengeance. All I knew I was being held up, torn in more than one direction, no time to line up. The corrupt had me face another cover up. Where the only way I could undo was face another review.

It was to create a challenge and skip the corrupts method right through. I was wondering who to face where to condition that final mission, and how to embrace, that next case. It had me forced to hit back with remorse and create a challenge to state and new fact and take it to the next level.

I was taught a lesson, left to hit back with redemption, repeating another competition. What a joke I had to evoke just to prove I was innocent. In true fact they knew what will happen next, because they created that test. An instigation that was interrogating me and have me face another voyage.

It followed up by an investigation, faced a tremor, from that vendetta. It served me a free will in the end; it made me sick and gave the corrupt a chance to fail me and hand out a prediction that led me towards a path of no return. They took me in and faced me in advance, so I never dance.

Just to have me walk the plank and run the end of my tremor delaying me at every terror. As if the road I was on had me on the wrong end helping the corrupt return and start again. As I was their constant punishment hitting me with a free ride. Serving me a challenge that had me face my truth.

I come first, with an everlasting fight. A demon who stalled, long enough to spread his semen. Planting seeds in the most awkward spaces, creating an energy that served me a will, just to hit back with a certain skill. A task to force me to revive a dive, a method used to reclaim dignity.

My faith, to humanity, lost hope and reality. It had come to a hold up because I was given a challenge that had me soldier through hitting me with a dignified clue. It was as if I grew up overnight nothing I gradually accrued through the years had purpose. For the method was a test to help me rise above.

Those who used me to get there. were purely fragments of my imagination. Added with a served purpose. In fact, I was given a trace to get back on track and face another rude awakening. The only thing that had me forgiving, was the action that had me return and hit back with the same reaction.

I had been taken for granted, left to repeat, test the patience of those who hit me ran and assume the outcome will hand them another winning streak. I was left to hit a trace a given reason to break the corrupts mission. I was a fool to let it get to me; it was only way I could walk that plank.

I was to push myself towards the next destination releasing that demon. A journey abetted, by a final reservation. Whereas if my wing was truly clipped, then the lie to harm me to take over, so I never get by or believe in myself. Would evidently be, and I would be withstanding in a benevolent sin.

AMEN

To be Continued

ABOUT THE AUTHOR

Panagiota Makaronis

I studied for my Bachelor of Arts and Bachelor of Commerce majoring in Philosophy and Theology at ACU Australian Catholic University. I also have a diploma in Clinical Hypnotherapy from Sterling Institute and The Australian Academy of Hypnotic Science.

My studies included Psychology, Neurolinguistic Programming, (N.L.P). Meditation, and Spirituality. Over the years I have worked with many clients where I delved into Mediumship Clairvoyancy Astrology Numerology Reiki and Crystal Healing.

I was on a mission of oppression, to study the human

mind and see in hindsight what makes people in society click.

I was so interested in Anthropology and Sociology, I had a lot of questions unanswered, so I decided to follow a path of the unknown to see how I can make sense of my reality.

My clients were, experimental to me. I was on a mission to investigate human nature and I met a lot of interesting people along the way.

Because I was quite accurate in my craft, I had several who became quite defensive. They could not wait to cover up their mess by challenging me, because they assumed I had a knowing, they could delete and delay me; by denying me access. All by attempting to harm my success.

That made my life quite interesting, it helped me with my writing. I had adventures, where I could sense I was on a path of defending my Honor. While others were hiding behind the truth, I was challenging it. Lucky for me I felt that I was being protected by my spirit along the way, where the Guidance from within never led me astray.

I had to take an absence of leave, because of family commitments, I went on a Sabbatical, decided to go back to university get my degree, clear my path, start fresh and bring myself back to reality.

I was fighting a lost cause, living another person's life, which lead me towards a destination where I could no longer lie to myself.

During my absence of leave, I went on a path of journalism and freelance writing, to broaden my Horizon, and to warn those who are inspired by the truth to set it all free and believe that dreams do come true.

Not only believe in yourself but in life, because life is too short, My Philosophy is not to follow others or worry about what others think neither. In the end, you have to live within yourself. Face your fears and trust your instincts. Because no one really knows what is around the corner.

No one knows unless you stick to the plan and even then, your world can collapse, and you have to start again. I should know! I have passed several paths, where my foundation was not strong enough to hold me, and it would collapse where I would have to rebuild again.

Having said that, you must remain positive, for time does not stand still, time is of the essence. Based on how much you can achieve in one lifetime, just to leave your Legacy Behind.

I strongly believe you must follow your path and how it might look to others it should not matter. As long as you can accept who you are then anything is possible.

Where in the end, I believe the right presentation will lead you to the right destination if you persevere.

AMEN

THE THEATRICAL MELODIA OF MY LIFE : CHRONICLE ONE

This book is based on my journey, the roller coaster I call life, my thought patterns, and my experiences. How I overcome so many turmoils, how I changed my perception, for it led me towards a destination that gave me tension. Where I felt I had no freedom or free will; all I had was failure. Added with faith, and the hope to overcome another fall. Feeding off the concept as I rise above it all!

The Lioness Of Judah A Metaphor Of Strength, Misjudgment, & Truth: Chronicle 31

My Philosophy "This is my metaphor the language of a burden, not reality."; it is my way of dealing with the pressure of what Civilization has to offer. My way, of letting Humanity know; what I perceive is what I believe.

The Luminous Fire Of Discretion:

Chronicle 30

A malicious cycle of events betrayed my trust. The scandal that put me on a journey that stirred everyone who was part of that contract. For those who assumed the road I chose was there's to consume, all by leading me on.

Devine Magnetism Awakening The Sovereign Soul: Chronicle 29

I was back on track stepping onto a new plane of awareness, after hitting a hold up, a knot I needed to break free from. The only way to do so was take a gamble. Only to arrive at a new state of being for the risk I took; has now paid off.

B3stow™ Admonished; A Doctrine Of Defiance: Chronicle 28

The adventures continue, my journey up to now was a fight; with who? Only the corrupt knew. An assumption from within, made me see clearly, I was not wrong; my intuition did not serve me wrong. I felt my privacy was being invaded.

The rumours continued, those who were in on it were supposedly; knights in shining armour.

The Temple Of Zeal: Chronicle 27

A renewal, to ground me from an old wound. My attention to detail brought redemption. I could sense my reality changing, from recovery into deception. Returning to hit back with passion; burnt out. Releasing the demon; as I pause an effect.

Leaving me once again stagnant to my development.

www.ingramcontent.com/pod-product-compliance
Lightning Source LLC
LaVergne TN
LVHW012332100826
845148LV00017B/2129

* 9 7 8 1 7 6 4 4 5 8 1 5 3 *